DON'T INTERRUPT ME,
I'm Talking To God!

90-Day Morning Prayer Devotional

Dear Evette,

Thank you for being the vessel of
honor that you are. You are an overcomer,
more than a conqueror, able to do all
things through christ. I pray
Ephisians 3:20 over your life. May
God do as it says in Amos 9:13
for things to happen rapidly.

Tiwana L. Adams

Blessings and peace

Tiwana L. Adams

Don't Interrupt Me, I'm Talking To God!

90-Day Morning Prayer Devotional

Copyright © 2021 Tiwana L. Adams

ISBN: 978-1-953535-21-4

Printed in the United States of America

Dedication

Too often, we don't express to people how much they inspire us to carry out our purpose in the earth, so I want to offer this dedication:

First, I give thanks to God for this book and for every daily prayer he has inspired.

Next, to the high priest of my home, my husband, my best friend, and the love of my life, Frank. I am grateful to God for anointing and sending him to find me. He is a special man to encourage and support all that I do and share me with all the prayer partners I connect with daily.

Also, to my third and fourth heartbeats, Frank III and Jalen, for being fine, respectful young men who represent their parents well and understand the power of prayer. This journey started when they were babies, and I've learned so much about having a relationship with Father God by parenting them. The learning continues while parenting them as adults, allowing a glimpse of what God sees in us as we grow and mature spiritually.

Finally, I dedicate this book to all of my blood and spiritual family members for being in my corner. God has provided me with an amazing tribe.

Acknowledgements

Along with three other writing projects, this book had been resting in me for the past three years. Then I received a prophetic nudge through a sermon I heard on Facebook Live. The speaker laid down a fifteen-day challenge, and I took it up and sat all day with the Lord and my computer to finish the work. Thank you, God, for sending that message on time through that man of God.

Since the release of my first book, *Uninterrupted Talks with God*, I've felt a great urging and ongoing encouragement from several people to share what's inside of me. The greatest push within me has come from the influence of my grandmother, Beatrice (Queen Bea). She was a strong, unstoppable woman who married only one man, gave birth to thirteen children, raised me as number fourteen, lived as a widow for thirty-five years, and remained a virtuous woman until she passed at ninety-five years young. All my life, I watched her make things happen. Anyone who knew my grandmother can see where I get my work ethic from.

She was the oldest of four children with parents who split up early in her childhood. As a young girl, she had to take on responsibilities in the home and help her mother work for provisions, which did not allow her to complete school. At age twenty-three, she wed my grandfather, and they remained married until he passed away thirty-seven years later.

In all my years, I never heard her murmur about having to work or take care of anyone. But she always worked hard, took care of sick family members, had several surgeries and ailments, and buried her husband and five of her children, but she didn't complain. Because of her upbringing, she prayed and worked with my grandfather to build a life and family, and God blessed them. She was a good steward over what God had given her.

When I think about that lady, I press on to do everything God has put in me to do. Unfortunately, my grandmother didn't live to see this book get completed. The Lord called her home a few months ago. She left gracefully even in death, taking her last breath while calling on the Lord.

I am grateful to God for sharpening me through the many people he has positioned in my life. My family always challenges me to go higher and do more. They never let me give up.

God has also allowed me to have some remarkable friends who love him almost more than I do. We hold one another accountable to finish our God-given assignments, and we share insights and information with one another to help us complete those assignments with excellence. I thank God for the push (like it or not) from Frank, Vernell, Stephanie, Latangela, Nellie, and Cheryle.

Introduction

At times, we experience what seem to be interruptions in our relationship with God and feel that we cannot accomplish or produce what he has spoken for our lives. When these interruptions occur, it feels almost like we're in a barren state, incapable of reproducing. According to the Merriam-Webster Online Dictionary, *interrupt* means "to stop or hinder by breaking in; to break the uniformity or continuity of." Interruptions take place all the time in our lives, diverting our attention and focus from accomplishing something. When these distractions come, our productivity in completing tasks decreases. All of us experience interruptions at some point in our day.

In regard to interruptions in our relationship with God, Satan comes at us first in the mind to temporarily paralyze our thoughts and ability to advance forward to the place God has for us. Actions such as prayer, fasting, and reading the word of God are often interrupted by the enemy because they strengthen us and build us up. The enemy does not want to let go of us when we seek to know the truth that makes us free. When we persevere and complete those activities, God gives us answers, revelation, deliverance, healing, and more power. That's why the fight feels so intense during those times.

Some years ago, my appetite increased for God's Word, prayer, and righteous living. In that process, the Lord called me to a higher place in the areas of prayer and fasting, intercession for others, and the time I spent in his word to gain greater understanding of what he was teaching me in practical ways. Now, I have to pause and say: be careful what you ask God for. He will give it to you, but likely not by way of a route you would pick. You will experience opposition in the process of growth. How well do I know this myself? I have been in nineteen accidents during my forty-nine years of life. Yet I have never broken a bone, and I've remained faithful in my posture of prayer and intercession no matter how much physical or emotional pain I felt—because I recognized that the enemy was sending interruptions during those times. But God knows in advance the plan for the fulfillment of the desires he has placed in each of us.

God has shown us through the witness of his word how to handle the interruptions that will surely come in our relationship with him. For example, Hannah was one of two wives to Elkanah. She remained barren, and Elkanah's other wife, Peninnah, provoked Hannah daily for being childless. In 1 Samuel 1-2, we see how part of God's plan was to navigate Hannah to her true place of purpose: intercession. This beautiful story shows how Hannah took a bumpy, somewhat unpleasant journey filled with interruptions in her life, but ultimately arrived at her place of destiny—with some bonuses for the trouble she went through. So, by looking at Hannah's example, we can remind ourselves first of all that God will do the same for us because of his love toward us.

In reading the story of Hannah, we must also remember that she lived in a time when it was shameful for a woman to be barren and thus unable to reproduce and give her husband a male child or other children to work the land. Hannah, though, remained a woman committed to God despite the Lord shutting her womb. Interrupted by thoughts of inadequacy, humiliation, and doubt, Hannah wept. She would not eat and she felt bitter in her soul. She retreated alone to the temple to be with the Lord and to worship and pray. Again, we can look to Hannah's example and remind ourselves that when we are experiencing interruptions and challenges in life, we must continue to seek a relationship with God through worship and by remaining in a humble posture to invite him to move in and through us.

Finally, we see in Hannah's story that she went to the temple to have an uninterrupted talk with God, but then the priest Eli interrupted her conversation with God. Sometimes the very people we think should be most protective of our relationship with God can themselves be disruptive and get in the way, causing us to neglect our time with him because of their interruptions. Hannah was praying for a change in her situation, but Israel's spiritual leader had no idea what she was doing, nor did he have any sensitivity to her posture of prayer. She desired for her barren womb to wake up and produce a male child to be dedicated back to the Lord, and so she made a vow to give a son back to God for the rest of his life. God heard and honored her prayer, opened her womb, and gave her a son whom she named Samuel. Not only did God grant her request for a son, but he opened her womb to birth five more children. As seen in Hannah's life, when we remain focused and continue to talk with God, he will honor and respond to our requests.

On this 90-day journey, I challenge you to pray the prayers, to let the scriptures speak to you, and to allow the stimulating thoughts to provoke you to think things through from God's perspective. Write out what you are thinking at that moment between the sentences, in the margins, or in the space provided for reflections. Take authority over your time and be intentional about having a conversation with God. Be bold enough to tell whoever attempts to snatch that time, "DON'T INTERRUPT ME, I'M TALKING TO GOD!"

Day 1

Great morning, God. Great morning, Jesus. Great morning, Holy Spirit. Thank you, God, for this day that you have made, and we are glad and rejoicing in it. Forgive us, God, for the things we have said, done, thought, and felt that are not pleasing to you nor lining up with your word.

Lord, you keep on blessing us as you wake us up each morning with a right mind and still breathing air. Ignite us today as we get excited about your goodness and all that you have for us. What you have for us is for us only. We call forth everything that you have designated to take place and come to pass in our lives.

Your word fills a void according to Proverbs 24:3-16: *"Through wisdom is an house builded; and by understanding it is established: and by knowledge shall the chambers be filled with all precious and pleasant riches. A wise man is strong; yea, a man of knowledge increaseth strength. For by wise counsel thou shalt make thy war: and in multitude of counsellors there is safety. Wisdom is too high for a fool: he openeth not his mouth in the gate. He that deviseth to do evil shall be called a mischievous person. The thought of foolishness is sin: and the scorner is an abomination to men. If thou faint in the day of adversity, thy strength is small. If thou forbear to deliver them that are drawn unto death, and those that are*

1

ready to be slain; if thou sayest, Behold, we knew it not; doth not he that pondereth the heart consider it? and he that keepeth thy soul, doth not he know it? and shall not he render to every man according to his works? My son, eat thou honey, because it is good; and the honeycomb, which is sweet to thy taste: so shall the knowledge of wisdom be unto thy soul: when thou hast found it, then there shall be a reward, and thy expectation shall not be cut off. Lay not wait, O wicked man, against the dwelling of the righteous; spoil not his resting place: For a just man falleth seven times, and riseth up again: but the wicked shall fall into mischief."

Thank you, God, for accomplishments being made today as we follow your direction to complete assignments. Even when we fail in our attempts, your plan far exceeds our ways of getting things done. There is purpose behind everything that comes out of what we do, so give us the patience to wait on you for a response. It is in the name of Jesus that we do pray with thanksgiving. Amen.

Stimulating Thought

Remain positive in everything that you say, think, and do, for God is always listening and watching. Even when others do you wrong, vengeance belongs to God and he will take care of those individuals. Pray for them to be blessed, because sometimes they may have areas of void or hurt in their lives that cause them to become bitter and display it toward others who have done nothing to them. Press in for the love of God dwelling in you to be what draws them back to the place of safety and away from the clutches of Satan. Remember that God has your back no matter what it may look like or how you may feel.

Reflections

_____

_____

_____

_____

_____

_____

_____

Day 2

Great morning, God. Great morning, Jesus. Great morning, Holy Spirit. Thank you, God, for this day that you have made, and we are glad and rejoicing in it. Forgive us, God, for the things we have said, done, thought, and felt that are not pleasing to you nor lining up with your word.

We have another day to take the journey of impacting your kingdom, and we are glad to have this opportunity. Humble our hearts to do your will with joy, Father God. We yield ourselves to you and do all things as to the Lord. Draw us close to you and reveal those hidden things you desire for us to know. Give each of us a praying spirit, God, to pray your heart and mind. Purify our hearts and minds so that we will be usable vessels. Remove the barriers that arise as a result of issues of the heart.

Help us to make wise choices based on your standards of holy living, rather than the world's standards. Let our lives display the character of wisdom according to Proverbs 19:1-21: *"Better is the poor that walketh in his integrity, than he that is perverse in his lips, and is a fool. Also, that the soul be without knowledge, it is not good; and he that hasteth with his feet sinneth. The foolishness of man perverteth his way: and his heart fretteth against the Lord. Wealth maketh many friends; but the poor is separated from his neighbor. A false witness shall not be unpunished, and he that speaketh lies shall not escape. Many will entreat the favour of the prince: and every man is a friend to him that giveth gifts. All the brethren of the poor do hate him: how much more do his friends go far from him? he pursueth them with words, yet they are wanting to him. He that getteth wisdom loveth his own soul: he that keepeth understanding shall find good. A false witness shall not be unpunished, and he that speaketh lies shall perish. Delight is not seemly for a fool; much less for a servant to have rule over princes. The discretion of a man deferreth his anger; and it is his glory to pass over a transgression. The king's wrath is as the roaring of a lion; but his favour is as dew upon the grass. A foolish son is the calamity of his father: and the contentions of a wife are a continual dropping. House and riches are the inheritance of fathers: and a prudent wife is from the Lord. Slothfulness casteth into a deep sleep; and an idle soul shall suffer hunger. He that keepeth the commandment keepeth his own soul; but he that despiseth his ways shall die. He that hath pity upon the poor lendeth unto the Lord; and that which he hath given will he pay him again. Chasten thy son while there is hope, and let not thy soul spare for his crying. A man of great wrath shall suffer punishment: for if thou deliver him, yet thou must do it again. Hear counsel, and receive instruction, that thou mayest be wise in thy latter end. There are many devices in a man's heart; nevertheless the counsel of the Lord, that shall stand."*

Let us be so rooted in your word that our lives will be the word made alive. We command our day to prosper and be well balanced among body, mind, and spirit with every task that we perform. There will be nothing out of alignment today, for we are in step with your master plan. It is in the name of Jesus that we do pray. Amen.

Stimulating Thought

Make choices today that will propel you to a brighter future and to make an impact in the kingdom. If a choice does not make sense and will not improve your life or the lives of others, don't pursue it. We know how cunning Satan can be to send thoughts and make something seem good initially, but in the long run, it will have devastating effects on your life and also make you feel guilty about the choice you made. The blessings of the Lord make us rich and do not add sorrow to our lives. Although something may seem to be a blessing, who is it really coming from: God or Satan? As our soul prospers, God gets glory out of it all. When we take credit for what we have gained, did God do it? Proceed by making the best choice and by taking the route that God would have you go to arrive there.

Reflections

Day 3

Great morning, God. Great morning, Jesus. Great morning, Holy Spirit. Thank you, God, for this day that you have made, and we are glad and rejoicing in it. Forgive us, God, for the things we have said, done, thought, and felt that are not pleasing to you nor lining up with your word.

It is another day that you have kept us from the clutches of the enemy and have not allowed him to take us out. Thank you for life, health, and strength. You have given us joy and peace that we are thankful for. In the midst of all the busy things going on in this world, you are still God, working things out for our good.

We pray today for salvation in the lives of the lost wandering aimlessly each day with no direction. Deliver the captives bound by forces beyond their capability to break free from. You are the all-wise and all-knowing God, able to do anything but fail. When we temporarily stray from the path of righteousness, you still love us enough to bring us back to where we need to be instead of leaving us unprotected outside of your "ark" of safety.

Touch our hearts to pray for and assist a brother or sister when we see them in need spiritually, emotionally, or physically. We are our brother's and sister's keeper when we see a need in their lives. Help us to display the character according to the word in Acts 20:32-38: *"And now, brethren, I commend you to God, and to the word of his grace, which is able to build you up, and to give you an inheritance among all them which are sanctified. I have coveted no man's silver, or gold, or apparel. Yea, ye yourselves know, that these hands have ministered unto my necessities, and to them that were with me. I have shewed you all things, how that so labouring ye ought to support the weak, and to remember the words of the Lord Jesus, how he said, It is more blessed to give than to receive. And when he had thus spoken, he kneeled down, and prayed with them all. And they all wept sore, and fell on Paul's neck, and kissed him, sorrowing most of all for the words which he spake, that they should see his face no more. And they accompanied him unto the ship."*

Give us a heart for ministry, God, and not a spirit of just gaining what we can for ourselves. God, you have shown us that there is much work to do in the kingdom and that we can all participate by helping one another. Take away any competitive jealous spirit that would rise up within us so that we may cover more ground in the kingdom together instead of separately, as man would rise to shine instead of you getting the glory. We thank you in advance, for it is already done. In the mighty name of Jesus we do pray. Amen.

Stimulating Thought

Spend more time taking inventory of your own life for any possible areas of improvement instead of inventorying the lives of others. Although God has given us the ability and freedom to form our own opinions, he is not interested in our thoughts concerning the lives of others. He desires for each of us to have a pure heart and clean hands and to walk in obedience to the word. Start today with action steps to implement these things in your life if you do not already have them in place.

Reflections

_____

_____

_____

_____

_____

_____

_____

Day 4

Great morning, God. Great morning, Jesus. Great morning, Holy Spirit. Thank you, God, for this day that you have made, and we are glad and rejoicing in it. Forgive us, God, for the things we have said, done, thought, and felt that are not pleasing to you nor lining up with your word.

Thank you, God, for waking us up this morning with a right mind and focused on you. Give us clarity in what we hear and see today as you guide us in all things we do. Set our agenda for the day and only open the windows of opportunity to complete the tasks intended for us. Keep us well balanced in body, mind, and spirit, so that we do not give more weight to one area over another. Broaden our vocabulary to only release words that will produce life, healing, and prosperity. Erase our memories of all the hurt, disappointment, and shame that cripple us from advancing. Propel us to the next level of performance so that we will not function below our capable range of excellence. We realize that nothing just happens by accident or happenchance in our lives, but is a result of our choices. Thank you for what you allow in our lives for us to grow and to get through the process for our lives.

Help us to think on your word at all times when making decisions about our personal affairs, as it says in Proverbs 28:6-28 (NIV): *"Better the poor whose walk is blameless than the rich whose ways are perverse. A discerning son heeds instruction, but a companion of gluttons disgraces his father. Whoever increases wealth by taking interest or profit from the poor amasses it for another, who will be kind to the poor. If anyone turns a deaf ear to my instruction, even their prayers are detestable. Whoever leads the upright along an evil path will fall into their own trap, but the blameless will receive a good inheritance. The rich are wise in their own eyes; one who is poor and discerning sees how deluded they are. When the righteous triumph, there is great elation; but when the wicked rise to power, people go into hiding. Whoever conceals their sins does not prosper, but the one who confesses and renounces them finds mercy. Blessed is the one who always trembles before God, but whoever hardens their heart falls into trouble. Like a roaring lion or a charging bear is a wicked ruler over a helpless people. A tyrannical ruler practices extortion, but one who hates ill-gotten gain will enjoy a long reign. Anyone tormented by the guilt of murder will seek refuge in the grave; let no one hold them back. The one whose walk is blameless is kept safe, but the one whose ways are perverse will fall into the pit. Those who work their land will have abundant food, but those who chase fantasies will have their fill of poverty. A faithful person will be richly blessed, but one eager to get rich will not go unpunished. To show partiality is not good—yet a person will do wrong for a piece of bread. The stingy are eager to get rich and are unaware that poverty awaits them. Whoever rebukes a person will in the end gain favor rather than one who has a flattering tongue. Whoever robs their father or mother and says, 'It's not wrong,' is partner to one who destroys. The greedy stir up conflict, but those who trust in the Lord will prosper. Those who trust in themselves are fools, but those who walk in wisdom are kept safe. Those who give to the poor will lack nothing, but those who close their eyes to them receive many curses. When the wicked rise to power, people go into hiding; but when the wicked perish, the righteous thrive."*

Make us great stewards and wise servants. Purify our hearts and thoughts to do what is right unto you and on behalf of others. Open the windows of heaven and pour out your blessing until there is not room enough for us to receive it so that we will have to sow generously into the kingdom. Blow winds of change through our nation to truly be the *United* States of America. Let unity flow from coast to coast and all around the world, that love and peace would rest in the hearts of humanity. In the name of Jesus we do pray. Amen.

Stimulating Thought

Open your heart and your hands to release into the lives of others what can be shared. When things are closed, it is just as hard for something to enter in. Consider today how you may contribute to improve your own life and the lives of others. As we take steps to do good to others, the returns will come in our own lives. God smiles upon the cheerful giver—not just the giver of money, but also of time and dedication. Do things with intent and on purpose.

Reflections

_____

_____

_____

_____

_____

_____

_____

Day 5

Great morning, God. Great morning, Jesus. Great morning, Holy Spirit. Thank you, God, for this day that you have made, and we are glad and rejoicing in it. Forgive us, God, for the things we have said, done, thought, and felt that are not pleasing to you nor lining up with your word.

Thank you for a time to exhale all the things that have been inhaled into our spirits, now just sitting there and waiting to be released. Hebrews 4:2-16 tells us: *"For unto us was the gospel preached, as well as unto them: but the word preached did not profit them, not being mixed with faith in them that heard it. For we which have believed do enter into rest, as he said, As I have sworn in my wrath, if they shall enter into my rest: although the works were finished from the foundation of the world. For he spake in a certain place of the seventh day on this wise, and God did rest the seventh day from all his works. And in this place again, If they shall enter into my rest. Seeing therefore it remaineth that some must enter therein, and they to whom it was first preached entered not in because of unbelief: again, he limiteth a certain day, saying in David, To day, after so long a time; as it is said, To day if ye will hear his voice, harden not your hearts. For if Jesus had given them rest, then would he not afterward have spoken of another day. There remaineth therefore a rest to the people of God. For he that is entered into his rest, he also hath ceased from his own works, as God did from his. Let us labour therefore to enter into that rest, lest any man fall after the same example of unbelief. For the word of God is quick, and powerful, and sharper than any twoedged sword, piercing even to the dividing asunder of soul and spirit, and of the joints and marrow, and is a discerner of the thoughts and intents of the heart. Neither is there any creature that is not manifest in his sight: but all things are naked and opened unto the eyes of him with whom we have to do. Seeing then that we have a great high priest, that is passed into the heavens, Jesus the Son of God, let us hold fast our profession. For we have not an high priest which cannot be touched with the feeling of our infirmities; but was in all points tempted like as we are, yet without sin. Let us therefore come boldly unto the throne of grace, that we may obtain mercy, and find grace to help in time of need."*

Teach us to rest in you because rest is good for our spirits and bodies. You incorporated rest into your week of creating the earth and intend for us to rest as well. Take away the anxiety that tries to fill us, because we know you always deliver on time what is needed for our lives. Give us wisdom to know when to back away and say no to some assignments and requests that are not intended for us. In Jesus's name we pray. Amen.

Stimulating Thought

Embrace your life at this moment, not despising where you are. Everything happens for a reason at the time it happens, so don't second-guess the choices you have made or the paths you have taken. God has allowed those things for the plan he has set for your life. Rest in him without overthinking situations.

Reflections

_____

_____

_____

_____

_____

_____

_____

Day 6

Great morning, God. Great morning, Jesus. Great morning, Holy Spirit. Thank you, God, for this day that you have made, and we are glad and rejoicing in it. Forgive us, God, for the things we have said, done, thought, and felt that are not pleasing to you nor lining up with your word.

Your unfailing love has once again lifted us up this morning for another day of life that you have breathed into us. Thank you for salvation through the blood of Jesus, which has redeemed us and reconnected us with you. We yield to your call and obey the set of instructions you have for us. This day we choose to serve you, Lord, as we give our whole heart to you. Our hearts, minds, and souls belong to you for the high price you paid on Calvary. Let the words of our mouths and the meditations of our hearts be acceptable in your sight and to your ears.

Restore, refresh, and rejuvenate us today in the areas of our lives where needed. You have given us keys to access everything we have need of in the kingdom. Matthew 16:18-21 tells us: *"And I say also unto thee, That thou art Peter, and upon this rock I will build my church; and the gates of hell shall not prevail against it. And I will give unto thee the keys of the kingdom of heaven: and whatsoever thou shalt bind on earth shall be bound in heaven: and whatsoever thou shalt loose on earth shall be loosed in heaven. Then charged he his disciples that they should tell no man that he was Jesus the Christ. From that time forth began Jesus to shew unto his disciples, how that he must go unto Jerusalem, and suffer many things of the elders and chief priests and scribes, and be killed, and be raised again the third day."*

We bind every foul, unclean spirit now in the name of Jesus, and we loose blessings and peace right now in the name of Jesus. There is power in the blood of Jesus and in his name, neither of which will ever lose strength. We decree and declare that the favor of the Lord rests upon our lives even as miracles, signs, and wonders follow after us. It is in the mighty name of Jesus that we say it is so. Amen.

Stimulating Thought

There is something to be thankful for every day because God said that we should give thanks in all things. You have the ability to command your day to be what God says it can be by speaking in faith those things that are not as though they were. Life and death are upon your tongue, so what will you believe God for? Speak life over your spiritual growth, physical health, and the prospering of your finances. Watch God respond to your faith.

Reflections

_____

_____

_____

_____

_____

Day 7

Great morning, God. Great morning, Jesus. Great morning, Holy Spirit. Thank you, God, for this day that you have made, and we are glad and rejoicing in it. Forgive us, God, for the things we have said, done, thought, and felt that are not pleasing to you nor lining up with your word.

God, we thank you for another day that you have blessed us to see. With hearts of thanksgiving, we give you praise today. Thank you for the ability to breathe, speak, walk, talk, and think. We are blessed with so many wonderful things each day, and we just want to acknowledge you in the midst of it all. We cannot go further in this day without giving you the necessary praise, God.

The greatest way we can thank you is to love one another. You have shown us unfailing love, so increase the love we possess toward others to be unconditional, unlimited, and sincere. Connect us with the people we need to be joined with for an impartation to take place. Just like we need you, God, we need others in our lives to survive, because we are joints fit together to supply what is needed for the whole body to function properly. Thank you for reminding us of your love for us according to your word in John 15:9-19: *"As the Father hath loved me, so have I loved you: continue ye in my love.*

If ye keep my commandments, ye shall abide in my love; even as I have kept my Father's commandments, and abide in his love. These things have I spoken unto you, that my joy might remain in you, and that your joy might be full. This is my commandment, That ye love one another, as I have loved you. Greater love hath no man than this, that a man lay down his life for his friends. Ye are my friends, if ye do whatsoever I command you. Henceforth I call you not servants; for the servant knoweth not what his lord doeth: but I have called you friends; for all things that I have heard of my Father I have made known unto you. Ye have not chosen me, but I have chosen you, and ordained you, that ye should go and bring forth fruit, and that your fruit should remain: that whatsoever ye shall ask of the Father in my name, he may give it you. These things I command you, that ye love one another. If the world hate you, ye know that it hated me before it hated you. If ye were of the world, the world would love his own: but because ye are not of the world, but I have chosen you out of the world, therefore the world hateth you."

Give us the grace today to offer soft answers and show exceeding love to those we interact with. Let every word from our mouths and the meditations of our hearts be acceptable to you, God. Let nothing negative or foul come from us that would potentially turn someone away from you. Let there be life in all that we say to encourage, build up, and exhort others. It is in the mighty name of Jesus that we do give thanks. Amen.

Stimulating Thought

Show love to all in every situation no matter who they are or what they have done. As you love, watch the hand of God move in all things. Even concerning those who use or mistreat you, watch the difference in their response as you love them and refuse to react to their behavior. As you are loving on others and God, thank him for giving you the strength to do so. God is well pleased with all that he has created. When he created you and me, he said, "It is good."

Remember you are good because God said so. Let that be the inspiration for you to do good.

Reflections

_____

_____

_____

_____

_____

_____

_____

Day 8

Great morning, God. Great morning, Jesus. Great morning, Holy Spirit. Thank you, God, for this day that you have made, and we are glad and rejoicing in it. Forgive us, God, for the things we have said, done, thought, and felt that are not pleasing to you nor lining up with your word.

God, we give you all glory this morning. You are an awesome God as you reign over all the earth. Thank you for your word being a light in our paths to usher us to the destinations where we need to go.

Thank you for life-changing wisdom according to Proverbs 15:13-33 (NASB): *"A joyful heart makes a cheerful face, but when the heart is sad, the spirit is broken. The mind of the intelligent seeks knowledge, but the mouth of fools feeds on foolishness. All the days of the needy are bad, but a cheerful heart has a continual feast. Better is a little with the fear of the Lord than great treasure, and turmoil with the treasure. Better is a portion of vegetables where there is love, than a fattened ox served with hatred. A hot-tempered man stirs up strife, but the slow to anger calms a dispute. The way of the lazy one is like a hedge of thorns, but the path of the upright is a highway. A wise son makes a father glad, but a foolish man despises his mother. Foolishness is joy to one who lacks sense, but a person of understanding walks straight. Without consultation, plans are frustrated, but with many counselors they succeed. A person has joy in an apt answer, and how delightful is a timely word! The path of life leads upward for the wise, so that he may keep away from Sheol below. The Lord will tear down the house of the proud, but He will set the boundary of the widow. Evil plans are an abomination to the Lord, but pleasant words are pure. He who profits illicitly troubles his own house, but he who hates bribes will live. The heart of the righteous ponders how to answer, but the mouth of the wicked pours out evil things. The Lord is far from the wicked, but He hears the prayer of the righteous. Bright eyes gladden the heart; good news refreshes the bones. One whose ear listens to a life-giving rebuke will stay among the wise. One who neglects discipline rejects himself, but one who listens to a rebuke acquires understanding. The fear of the Lord is the instruction for wisdom, and before honor comes humility."*

Tune our ears to hear the fullness of what you are speaking and not just the portions that appeal to our flesh. Discipline us to receive your words of truth when they are spoken and to live by them. We say "Have your way in us, Lord," because you do what is best for us, not what is convenient. Humble us and remove any residue of pride that would try to rise in us. Improve our living according to your standards and not those of man. God, we thank you for goodness and mercy in our lives every day. It is in the name of Jesus that we do pray. Amen.

Stimulating Thought

Make it a point to improve your life in some way each day. Be open to hear when others are giving helpful criticism that will bring positive change to your life. Listen to wise people and don't disregard advice they give when you see the results God has produced in their lives. Be open to change and not so stiff with old ways and traditions to get things done. Shift from the insanity of repeating actions that give the same results, and instead move to the unstoppable flow of increase as you open your mind and spirit to the exceeding things God will do through you if you will just let him.

Reflections

_____

_____

_____

_____

_____

_____

_____

Day 9

Great morning, God. Great morning, Jesus. Great morning, Holy Spirit. Thank you, God, for this day that you have made, and we are glad and rejoicing in it. Forgive us, God, for the things we have said, done, thought, and felt that are not pleasing to you nor lining up with your word.

We need your love today to embrace and cover every person we come in contact with. Stir up the evangelist inside each of us to share the good news with others today. Give us the grace to identify and walk in the purpose you have for our lives. Anoint us with fresh oil so that your presence will be felt with us every place we enter this day. Bring us to a place of peace, joy, and gladness as we obey you, your word, and your Holy Spirit.

Increase our desire for the word so that our hearts will be filled with it. Apply the word to our everyday living according to Proverbs 4:20-27: *"My son, attend to my words; incline thine ear unto my sayings. Let them not depart from thine eyes; keep them in the midst of thine heart. For they are life unto those that find them, and health to all their flesh. Keep thy heart with all diligence; for out of it are the issues of life. Put away from thee a froward mouth, and perverse lips put far from thee. Let thine eyes look right on, and let thine eyelids look straight before thee. Ponder the path of thy feet, and let all thy ways be established. Turn not to the right hand nor to the left: remove thy foot from evil."*

Open our spirits to receive as you impart. Strengthen us to resist the devil so that he will flee. Help us to make wise choices that will line up with your word and your will for our lives. Let us not lean on what we understand but instead acknowledge you in all of our ways to get revelation. It is in the name of Jesus we do pray. Amen.

Stimulating Thought

Apply your best listening skills to catch all that you need to take in today. It is not enough to just hear, because you might miss crucial information. As you listen, you are an active participant in the conversation. God is speaking to each of us every day, but we must train our ears in different settings to recognize when he begins to speak. Be effective and discerning where he has positioned you so that you know when to share what needs to be shared and when to just be quiet and pray. Every conversation or situation does not require making a statement or comment.

Reflections

_____

_____

_____

_____

_____

_____

_____

Day 10

Great morning, God. Great morning, Jesus. Great morning, Holy Spirit. Thank you, God, for this day that you have made, and we are glad and rejoicing in it. Forgive us, God, for the things we have said, done, thought, and felt that are not pleasing to you nor lining up with your word.

Impart wisdom in us this morning, Lord, to think, speak, and do what pleases you. Guard our hearts to remain pure and to release love even as you give love to us so freely. Teach us, Lord, how to love a right manner to bring about major change in devastating situations. Bring us into alignment and agreement with your word in all our ways and the decisions we make in life.

Help us, God, to obey and respect those who are in authority over us as you have indicated according to your word in Hebrews 13:1-17: *"Let brotherly love continue. Be not forgetful to entertain strangers: for thereby some have entertained angels unawares. Remember them that are in bonds, as bound with them; and them which suffer adversity, as being yourselves also in the body. Marriage is honourable in all, and the bed undefiled: but whoremongers and adulterers God will judge. Let your conversation be without covetousness; and be content with such things as ye have: for he hath said, I will never leave thee, nor forsake thee. So that we may boldly say, The Lord is my helper, and I will not fear what man shall do unto me. Remember them which have the rule over you, who have spoken unto you the word of God: whose faith follow, considering the end of their conversation. Jesus Christ the same yesterday, and to day, and for ever. Be not carried about with divers and strange doctrines. For it is a good thing that the heart be established with grace; not with meats, which have not profited them that have been occupied therein. We have an altar, whereof they have no right to eat which serve the tabernacle. For the bodies of those beasts, whose blood is brought into the sanctuary by the high priest for sin, are burned without the camp. Wherefore Jesus also, that he might sanctify the people with his own blood, suffered without the gate. Let us go forth therefore unto him without the camp, bearing his reproach. For here have we no continuing city, but we seek one to come. By him therefore let us offer the sacrifice of praise to God continually, that is, the fruit of our lips giving thanks to his name. But to do good and to communicate forget not: for with such sacrifices God is well pleased. Obey them that have the rule over you, and submit yourselves: for they watch for your souls, as they that must give account, that they may do it with joy, and not with grief: for that is unprofitable for you."*

Have mercy upon us all, Lord, for the things we do that violate what you have said in your word. Keep us from hypocritical ways of saying we live according to your word but then acting contrary to what it says. God, you have given us a standard to be holy because you are holy. Remove the excuses that we form in our minds to not be holy or to fully walk out a life of holiness. Give each of us a made-up mind that chooses to possess the fruit of the Spirit. Discipline us in our speech to not speak ill of one another. Let every word from our mouths and the meditations of our hearts be acceptable to you, God. It is in the name of Jesus that we pray and declare that your will be done. Amen.

Stimulating Thought

Be open to think on the good in every situation and not dwell on the bad. God instructs us to give thanks in all things, not just some things, and to think on the good things. Often, we become blinded by the negative things even when the good far exceeds the bad. Readjust your vision to view things in a different way. Each time a situation arises, begin to ask yourself, *How does God see this?* Think about it: God may be presenting an opportunity for growth. Something good comes out of every situation because God still gets glory. When we go through challenges, it always seems harder than when we finally experience the end result. Embrace what is taking place in your life because God has chosen you for the assignment.

Reflections

_____

_____

_____

_____

_____

_____

_____

Day 11

Great morning, God. Great morning, Jesus. Great morning, Holy Spirit. Thank you, God, for this day that you have made, and we are glad and rejoicing in it. Forgive us, God, for the things we have said, done, thought, and felt that are not pleasing to you nor lining up with your word.

Thank you for giving us thoughts of peace and not of sorrow or confusion. You keep us hidden in those times that trouble tries to rise. Purify our hearts to remain filled with love and joy, not holding on to any thoughts of bitterness. Thank you for your love that you show toward us when we do nothing to deserve it.

Keep us through the washing of your word as it tells us in Romans 5:1-11: *"Therefore being justified by faith, we have peace with God through our Lord Jesus Christ: by whom also we have access by faith into this grace wherein we stand, and rejoice in hope of the glory of God. And not only so, but we glory in tribulations also: knowing that tribulation worketh patience; and patience, experience; and experience, hope: and hope maketh not ashamed; because the love of God is shed abroad in our hearts by the Holy Ghost which is given unto us. For when we were yet without strength, in due time Christ died for the ungodly. For scarcely for a righteous man will one die:*

yet peradventure for a good man some would even dare to die. But God commendeth his love toward us, in that, while we were yet sinners, Christ died for us. Much more then, being now justified by his blood, we shall be saved from wrath through him. For if, when we were enemies, we were reconciled to God by the death of his Son, much more, being reconciled, we shall be saved by his life. And not only so, but we also joy in God through our Lord Jesus Christ, by whom we have now received the atonement."

Thank you, heavenly Father, that your bond of love is unbreakable. Condition our hearts to possess such love for you and others. Give us the patience to love as we should and to not make excuses for not loving or for thinking some people are not lovable. Thank you, God, for never turning your back on us but still encouraging us to go on in spite of our mistakes. In the name of Jesus we pray. Amen.

Stimulating Thought

Take time each morning to meditate on positive words of wisdom to start your day. The way you begin is often how you will finish. Beginning your morning by communicating with God to hear instructions for the day allows your day to go much more smoothly. Don't wait until things begin to go wrong before praying for the day to get better. Purpose in your heart that every day will be a great day no matter what happens. Appreciate every day that you live and breathe, because someone else might be wishing for the life you have.

Reflections

_____

_____

_____

Day 12

Great morning, God. Great morning, Jesus. Great morning, Holy Spirit. Thank you, God, for this day that you have made, and we are glad and rejoicing in it. Forgive us, God, for the things we have said, done, thought, and felt that are not pleasing to you nor lining up with your word.

Heal our spirits, bodies, minds, and finances so that we may be well balanced to serve you effectively. For any area out of alignment in our lives, bring it to the level it needs to be. If our spirits are soaring high but our physical bodies are weak and weary, give us wisdom to do the necessary work to get our bodies in shape. Check our thoughts and give us strength to cast down vain imaginations that cause us to think contrary to your word. Lord, we need you at all times: in good or bad, when happy or sad, while rich or poor, and during sickness and good health. You are still our God and we honor you.

Make us a praise in the earth for you today, and let it be ridiculous enough to get your attention. Give us an intense worship that will shift us to another realm of the Spirit for an encounter with you like never before. Your word comforts us according to Psalm 40:1-11: *"I waited patiently for the Lord; and he inclined unto me, and heard my cry. He brought me up also out of an horrible pit, out of the miry clay, and set my feet upon a rock, and established my goings. And he hath put a new song in my mouth, even praise unto our God: many shall see it, and fear, and shall trust in the Lord. Blessed is that man that maketh the Lord his trust, and respecteth not the proud, nor such as turn aside to lies. Many, O Lord my God, are thy wonderful works which thou hast done, and thy thoughts which are to us-ward: they cannot be reckoned up in order unto thee: if I would declare and speak of them, they are more than can be numbered. Sacrifice and offering thou didst not desire; mine ears hast thou opened: burnt offering and sin offering hast thou not required. Then said I, Lo, I come: in the volume of the book it is written of me, I delight to do thy will, O my God: yea, thy law is within my heart. I have preached righteousness in the great congregation: lo, I have not refrained my lips, O Lord, thou knowest. I have not hid thy righteousness within my heart; I have declared thy faithfulness and thy salvation: I have not concealed thy lovingkindness and thy truth from the great congregation. Withhold not thou thy tender mercies from me, O Lord: let thy loving-kindness and thy truth continually preserve me."*

Thank you for your peace that will not allow us to be moved prematurely from where we are supposed to be. We will see results as we remain calm and let you lead and guide us instead of advancing based on what would satisfy our flesh. We give you glory in all things. It is in the name of Jesus that we do pray. Amen.

Stimulating Thought

When the intensity of your struggles rises, press in and praise God even more. Satan knows what God has in store for you and wants to make you quit before obtaining the promise. The adversary desires to steal your joy, kill you, and destroy everything connected to you. If you throw in the towel and give up, he wins. The Bible already tells us that Satan is defeated. Since you already know his end, take pleasure in celebrating what you know will come to pass: victory!

Reflections

_____

_____

_____

_____

_____

_____

_____

Day 13

Great morning, God. Great morning, Jesus. Great morning, Holy Spirit. Thank you, God, for this day that you have made, and we are glad and rejoicing in it. Forgive us, God, for the things we have said, done, thought, and felt that are not pleasing to you nor lining up with your word.

Our souls love you, Jesus, and we just want to bless your name. Open our ears to hear what your Spirit speaks this morning as we prepare for this day. We accept the agenda you have set for us this day because all things will work out as we follow your lead. Guide our tongues and give us the grace and wisdom to say what is needed at the right time. Let us not speak out of turn while spewing negativity, poorly chosen words, or statements stemming from foolish thinking.

Sink your words into our spirits according to Hebrews 10:19-27 (NIV): *"Therefore, brothers and sisters, since we have confidence to enter the Most Holy Place by the blood of Jesus, by a new and living way opened for us through the curtain, that is, his body, and since we have a great priest over the house of God, let us draw near to God with a sincere heart and with the full assurance that faith brings, having our hearts sprinkled to cleanse us from a guilty conscience and having our bodies washed with pure water. Let us hold unswervingly to the hope we profess, for he who promised is faithful. And let us consider how we may spur one another on toward love and good deeds, not giving up meeting together, as some are in the habit of doing, but encouraging one another—and all the more as you see the Day approaching. If we deliberately keep on sinning after we have received the knowledge of the truth, no sacrifice for sins is left, but only a fearful expectation of judgment and of raging fire that will consume the enemies of God."*

Keep us in the fellowship among the saints so that we will pray one another through, sharpen each other, and build one another up. Give each of us a cheerful heart and a grateful spirit. Let no murmuring or complaints come from us, because we are blessed and highly favored. We pray today with thanksgiving in Jesus's name. Amen.

Stimulating Thought

Do not look to man for validation or approval. God already gave that to everyone. We have been justified and glorified by God because he knew us before he made us. Step out from the shadows of fear today because all things are possible with God and we can do what he has assigned. Keep your head up and don't look back. Continue to move forward, pressing toward the mark set before you. Greater days are ahead.

Reflections

_____

_____

_____

_____

_____

_____

Day 14

Great morning, God. Great morning, Jesus. Great morning, Holy Spirit. Thank you, God, for this day that you have made, and we are glad and rejoicing in it. Forgive us, God, for the things we have said, done, thought, and felt that are not pleasing to you nor lining up with your word.

We worship you this morning in the beauty of your holiness. When we think of your goodness and all that you have done and continue to do, we rejoice. Thank you for keeping us together in times when we feel like unraveling. Ignite us to get up and do something new to receive different results. Build our confidence and trust in your word to speak over every situation or scenario in life, no matter how big or small. There is nothing new taking place in the earth that your word will not address. Give us wisdom, understanding, and revelation of your word as we read and apply it to our daily living. Proverbs 4:1-7 directs us by saying: *"Hear, ye children, the instruction of a father, and attend to know understanding. For I give you good doctrine, forsake ye not my law. For I was my father's son, tender and only beloved in the sight of my mother. He taught me also, and said unto me, Let thine heart retain my words: keep my commandments, and live. Get wisdom, get understanding: forget it not; neither decline from the words of my mouth. Forsake her not, and she shall preserve thee: love her, and she shall keep thee. Wisdom is the principal thing; therefore get wisdom: and with all thy getting get understanding."*

We yield to you, Holy Spirit, and remain sensitive to what you are speaking. As we advance through this day, make us open and flexible when it is needed for a soul to be reached. Don't let us get caught up in self or our problems. We know you will take care of us, God, and we thank you. You are mighty and awesome today and forevermore. It is in the name of Jesus that we pray. Amen.

Stimulating Thought

In everything give thanks. Some things may not feel or look good in your life right now, but it is for your good in the long run. Everything has a place in the process. Don't try to avoid the necessary steps that will take you where you need to go. Taking shortcuts may force you to turn around and go back along the path you deviated from. Stay on course. You will have a greater appreciation for arriving at your destination once you have gone through all that you face along the way.

Reflections

_____

_____

_____

_____

_____

_____

_____

Day 15

Great morning, God. Great morning, Jesus. Great morning, Holy Spirit. Thank you, God, for this day that you have made, and we are glad and rejoicing in it. Forgive us, God, for the things we have said, done, thought, and felt that are not pleasing to you nor lining up with your word.

We are thankful today for the air that we breathe, a right mind stayed on Jesus, and good health in our bodies and spirits. We pray today for peace beyond understanding to all people. Give us wisdom in the choices we make about what we say, do, and think. Let us not lean on our own understanding but rather trust in the Lord with all our hearts, acknowledging him in all our ways to direct our paths. Open our minds to think on good things, not dwelling on the bad or our past. What already happened is done and we are advancing to improve the present moment. This will be a great day and nothing can alter what we command to come forth. Protect us from the violating thoughts and actions the enemy wants to impose on us. Guard our hearts against bitterness and corruption. Shield our spirits against becoming ground for negative or contaminated dumping. Build us up in our most holy faith as we come before you, always praying.

Holy Spirit, fill our vessels so that everything we release will positively reflect our heavenly Father. We honor your word according to 1 Thessalonians 5:12-24 (NIV): *"Now we ask you, brothers and sisters, to acknowledge those who work hard among you, who care for you in the Lord and who admonish you. Hold them in the highest regard in love because of their work. Live in peace with each other. And we urge you, brothers and sisters, warn those who are idle and disruptive, encourage the disheartened, help the weak, be patient with everyone. Make sure that nobody pays back wrong for wrong, but always strive to do what is good for each other and for everyone else. Rejoice always, pray continually, give thanks in all circumstances; for this is God's will for you in Christ Jesus. Do not quench the Spirit. Do not treat prophecies with contempt but test them all; hold on to what is good, reject every kind of evil. May God himself, the God of peace, sanctify you through and through. May your whole spirit, soul and body be kept blameless at the coming of our Lord Jesus Christ. The one who calls you is faithful, and he will do it."*

Thank you for the results that will come from our obedience. Let favor rest on those we are connected to simply because of the relationship formed among us in the spirit of unity and love. Do a quick work as you honor the supplications we make on behalf of others. It is in the name of Jesus that we do pray. Amen.

Stimulating Thought

Be watchful and pray. You don't have to accept things the way they are. You possess the power to choose life or death in situations. Take a stand and be firm. Do not waver in your decision to live right. Even if you have to be alone, just be right. Be determined and have a mind made up not to compromise in this hour. The stakes are too high to take that gamble. Someone is watching you all the time and following the example you are setting, especially when you would least expect it. Make a God impression upon the lives of others and come out with a winning hand.

Reflections

_____

_____

_____

_____

_____

_____

_____

Day 16

Great morning, God. Great morning, Jesus. Great morning, Holy Spirit. Thank you, God, for this day that you have made, and we are glad and rejoicing in it. Forgive us, God, for the things we have said, done, thought, and felt that are not pleasing to you nor lining up with your word.

Lord, we worship and adore your name today. Thank you for peace, joy, and love today. Keep our minds stayed on you and focused on the things we are doing. Slow us down from the busy lifestyles we so often live to instead make time for important things, like family, prayer, worship, and fellowship.

Build our foundations on firm footers so that we may have a firm and stable life in Christ. Thank you that 1 Corinthians 3:9-14 says: *"For we are labourers together with God: ye are God's husbandry, ye are God's building. According to the grace of God which is given unto me, as a wise masterbuilder, I have laid the foundation, and another buildeth thereon. But let every man take heed how he buildeth thereupon. For other foundation can no man lay than that is laid, which is Jesus Christ. Now if any man build upon this foundation gold, silver, precious stones, wood, hay, stubble; every man's work shall be made manifest: for the day shall declare it, because it shall be revealed by fire; and the fire shall try every man's work of what sort it is. If any man's work abide which he hath built thereupon, he shall receive a reward."*

We embrace this current season of life to be built up and fortified. Balance every aspect of our lives to withstand the trials and afflictions we will face. Keep us anchored so that we will not be tossed by the winds that blow in our lives. You will not place any more upon us than we can handle, so thank you for the strength that you have placed in us. It is in the name of Jesus that we do pray. Amen.

Stimulating Thought

Be prepared by creating a plan and then working that plan. Throughout the Bible, we find people going through a preparation period while God took them through a process for a great outcome. We are all a part of God's plan for something. Ask God what his plan for your life is, for he knows the plan. Listen to his response and then implement the things necessary in your life if you are not already functioning in what he has set for you. When we open ourselves to be taught, our greatest teacher is God. He has given his Holy Spirit to tutor us every day, but we must take time to receive what he desires to show us.

Reflections

_____

_____

_____

_____

_____

_____

_____

Day 17

Great morning, God. Great morning, Jesus. Great morning, Holy Spirit. Thank you, God, for this day that you have made, and we are glad and rejoicing in it. Forgive us, God, for the things we have said, done, thought, and felt that are not pleasing to you nor lining up with your word.

Give us pure hearts to love and serve in a manner that pleases you. Wake up the things inside of us that have been asleep and inactive for far too long. Time slows down for no one; neither does death stop seeking those it has an appointment with. Make us diligent individuals who will live our lives in the purpose set for us to acquire the promises that you made to each of us. Give us the zeal and courage to chase after you, God, no matter what trials may come. Keep us focused on the things concerning you, for you would have us serve one another rather than acquiring things for ourselves. We know you will take care of us, God, as we take care of your business.

Thank you for our daily bread as our spirits are fed by your word. Thank you for the stability that comes as we meditate on Psalm 5:1-12: *"Give ear to my words, O Lord, consider my meditation. Hearken unto the voice of my cry, my King, and my God: for unto thee will I pray. My voice shalt thou hear in the morning, O Lord; in the morning will I direct my prayer unto thee, and will look up. For thou art not a God that hath pleasure in wickedness: neither shall evil dwell with thee. The foolish shall not stand in thy sight: thou hatest all workers of iniquity. Thou shalt destroy them that speak leasing: the Lord will abhor the bloody and deceitful man. But as for me, I will come into thy house in the multitude of thy mercy: and in thy fear will I worship toward thy holy temple. Lead me, O Lord, in thy righteousness because of mine enemies; make thy way straight before my face. For there is no faithfulness in their mouth; their inward part is very wickedness; their throat is an open sepulchre; they flatter with their tongue. Destroy thou them, O God; let them fall by their own counsels; cast them out in the multitude of their transgressions; for they have rebelled against thee. But let all those that put their trust in thee rejoice: let them ever shout for joy, because thou defendest them: let them also that love thy name be joyful in thee. For thou, Lord, wilt bless the righteous; with favour wilt thou compass him as with a shield."*

We are open and yielded today for you to take us to higher heights and deeper depths. As we are drawn closer to you, make a significant change in us for others to see you in everything we say and do. Step up our evangelism to be fishers of men to draw them to Christ. Illuminate the light within us to radiate in dark places for truth to be seen and right direction to be taken. It is in the name of Jesus we do pray. Amen.

Stimulating Thought

Think on the good things that you have seen come from the lives of others. Speak life to revive every dying situation and to resurrect those things that are dead. There is more power inside us than we use sometimes. All we have to do is ask God and he will do it when we ask in Jesus's name. Are you courageous enough to ask?

Reflections

_____

_____

_____

_____

_____

_____

_____

Day 18

Great morning, God. Great morning, Jesus. Great morning, Holy Spirit. Thank you, God, for this day that you have made, and we are glad and rejoicing in it. Forgive us, God, for the things we have said, done, thought, and felt that are not pleasing to you nor lining up with your word.

Our souls love Jesus and bless his name. He is a wonder in our souls. God, you are omnipresent and we are thankful for your presence. You know our hearts and our very thoughts. Purify the thoughts we entertain. Cast down every vain imagination.

Continue to cover us wherever we are, as indicated in Psalm 139:1-10: *"O lord, thou hast searched me, and known me. Thou knowest my downsitting and mine uprising, thou understandest my thought afar off. Thou compassest my path and my lying down, and art acquainted with all my ways. For there is not a word in my tongue, but, lo, O Lord, thou knowest it altogether. Thou hast beset me behind and before, and laid thine hand upon me. Such knowledge is too wonderful for me; it is high, I cannot attain unto it. Whither shall I go from thy spirit? or whither shall I flee from thy presence? If I ascend up into heaven, thou art there: if I make my bed in hell, behold, thou art there. If I take the wings of the morning, and dwell in the uttermost parts of the sea; even there shall thy hand lead me, and thy right hand shall hold me."*

Shift us back on course when we have deviated from the path you have set for us to travel. Thank you for safe arrival at the destination we are to reach at the appointed time. Remove any desire in us to stop and watch what others are doing, thus stalling our own progress. It is in the name of Jesus that we pray. Amen.

Stimulating Thought

Life is like going to school. Every day there are lessons we can learn if we take note of what the instructor, the Holy Spirit, is teaching. Jesus is our administrator to ensure policies are fulfilled, because he tried them all out himself and knows firsthand the effects of following them, as well as results that come from obeying. God is our principal, the one to make sure the appropriate reward is given for living right—and the one to discipline unacceptable behavior. So every process you undergo is a test, mostly multiple choice, to see if you are learning what is being taught. The Father, Son, and Holy Spirit are all rooting for you to make it through life's requirements and to one day receive your diploma as God declares "Well done!" to you.

Reflections

Day 19

Great morning, God. Great morning, Jesus. Great morning, Holy Spirit. Thank you, God, for this day that you have made, and we are glad and rejoicing in it. Forgive us, God, for the things we have said, done, thought, and felt that are not pleasing to you nor lining up with your word.

Lord, we are thankful to you this day for all things. Thank you for allowing us to sleep last night and to rise for another day. We rejoice today for every ability you have given us: to breathe, think, move, and talk. So often we take for granted the smallest things we do all the time but, God, we just want to say, "Thank you." You are our deliverer even when we don't realize that deliverance is taking place. Continue to hold back the hand of the enemy from devouring our lives as he comes to steal, kill, and destroy us. Holy Ghost, have your way as you guide us on the path of righteousness where there is the least resistance and turmoil from the enemy.

Thank you for reminding us of your love for us in John 10:7-18: *"Then said Jesus unto them again, Verily, verily, I say unto you, I am the door of the sheep. All that ever came before me are thieves and robbers: but the sheep did not hear them. I am the door: by me if any man enter in, he shall be saved, and shall go in and out, and find pasture. The thief cometh not, but for to steal, and to kill, and to destroy: I am come that they might have life, and that they might have it more abundantly. I am the good shepherd: the good shepherd giveth his life for the sheep. But he that is an hireling, and not the shepherd, whose own the sheep are not, seeth the wolf coming, and leaveth the sheep, and fleeth: and the wolf catcheth them, and scattereth the sheep. The hireling fleeth, because he is an hireling, and careth not for the sheep. I am the good shepherd, and know my sheep, and am known of mine. As the Father knoweth me, even so know I the Father: and I lay down my life for the sheep. And other sheep I have, which are not of this fold: them also I must bring, and they shall hear my voice; and there shall be one fold, and one shepherd. Therefore doth my Father love me, because I lay down my life, that I might take it again. No man taketh it from me, but I lay it down of myself. I have power to lay it down, and I have power to take it again. This commandment have I received of my Father."*

Jesus, you paid it all for us, and we are thankful for what you took on for us. We accept the abundance that you arranged for us to have and for the love you have shown us. Thank you for not expecting repayment for what you have done, except to obey and love you.

Help us keep our hands to the plow as we remain anchored in you, Lord, with our minds set on you. We are free from any bondage that tries to hold us, because your word and Holy Spirit remind us each day that those whom the Son has freed are free indeed. It is in the name of Jesus that we pray. Amen.

Stimulating Thought

Slow down and take time for God while you can. Do not let life pass you by while staying too busy for God and then only spending time with him once your health has declined and you are forced to take it easy. God has need of you and appreciates all his creation, because he said it is good. As you take time with God, begin to rediscover the greatness he has placed within you.

Reflections

_____

_____

_____

_____

_____

_____

_____

Day 20

Great morning, God. Great morning, Jesus. Great morning, Holy Spirit. Thank you, God, for this day that you have made, and we are glad and rejoicing in it. Forgive us, God, for the things we have said, done, thought, and felt that are not pleasing to you nor lining up with your word.

Thank you, God, for being ever present in our lives, for we need you every hour. We rejoice in you today as we think of your goodness and all that you have done for us and what you continue to do each day. Let your glory rise among us, Lord. Open our mouths for praises to fill the atmosphere. We thank you for your grace, mercy, and peace resting upon us today. Everything you created is good, so we are excited about existing because you made us. You made us free when Jesus came to die, and for that we say, "Thank you."

The blood of Jesus is still as powerful as it was over two thousand years ago when the first drop came down. As 1 John 1:1-7 (NIV) emphasizes: *"That which was from the beginning, which we have heard, which we have seen with our eyes, which we have looked at and our hands have touched—this we proclaim concerning the Word of life. The life appeared; we have seen it and testify to it, and we proclaim to you the eternal life, which was with the Father and has appeared to us.*

We proclaim to you what we have seen and heard, so that you also may have fellowship with us. And our fellowship is with the Father and with his Son, Jesus Christ. We write this to make our joy complete. This is the message we have heard from him and declare to you: God is light; in him there is no darkness at all. If we claim to have fellowship with him and yet walk in the darkness, we lie and do not live out the truth. But if we walk in the light, as he is in the light, we have fellowship with one another, and the blood of Jesus, his Son, purifies us from all sin."

As we are purified from sin, thank you that there is no distinction between big sins and little sins. It is simply sin, no matter who commits it, when it happens, or where it is done, because it begins in our minds with a thought. Change our thinking today so that we will not welcome any suggestions from the devil. We cast down every vain imagination. Our thoughts remain on what is lovely and of good report. It is in the name of Jesus that we pray. Amen.

Stimulating Thought

Just as we should take care of our physical bodies with exercise, rest, and healthy food, our spirits require the same things. Read the word and meditate on it. Pray to the heavenly Father for him to speak back to your spirit. Fast when he says it is necessary to build you up. When your spirit is feeling weak and weary, you may need a dose of spiritual "vitamin C," so simply call on Jesus and he will give you what you need.

Reflections

_____

_____

_____

_____

_____

_____

_____

_____

_____

Day 21

Great morning, God. Great morning, Jesus. Great morning, Holy Spirit. Thank you, God, for this day that you have made, and we are glad and rejoicing in it. Forgive us, God, for the things we have said, done, thought, and felt that are not pleasing to you nor lining up with your word.

We are excited this morning as we think about you, Lord. You continue to bless us even when we have not done anything to deserve such blessings. Grace and mercy continue to cover our lives, and they are sufficient to get the job done. Our lives are in your hands, Lord, and we yield to the direction of your Holy Spirit. We glorify you for being the Most High God over the heavens and the earth. Thank you, God, for knowing all things that take place in the earth with every person, for nothing is hidden from you.

You are able to take care of each of our situations at the same time because of your awesomeness. We are thankful for your posture according to Psalm 93:1-5: *"The Lord reigneth, he is clothed with majesty; the Lord is clothed with strength, wherewith he hath girded himself: the world also is stablished, that it cannot be moved. Thy throne is established of old: thou art from everlasting. The floods have lifted up, O Lord, the floods have lifted up their voice; the floods lift up their waves. The Lord on high is mightier than the noise of many waters, yea, than the mighty waves of the sea. Thy testimonies are very sure: holiness becometh thine house, O Lord, for ever."*

Build our confidence today as we trust and depend on you for all things in our lives. Give each of us a thankful spirit as we rejoice in you for all things. We realize that our current place in life is because you have allowed us to arrive here, so we don't despise this place. Give us a greater appreciation for the lives of others and the purpose they have in our own lives. We love you, Jesus. We love ourselves and others because you made us all good. Thank you for your blessing, peace, and favor overtaking us today. In Jesus's name we pray. Amen.

Stimulating Thought

Consider that God handpicked the gifts and talents that he gave to you. Don't take lightly the ability he has given you. Gracefully use these gifts with care and diligence. Be disciplined when using your gifts, not abusing the power and authority that comes with them. They were given not only for you, but also to enhance the lives of others in some way. Allow yourself to be sharpened each day and God will get glory out of your life.

Reflections

_____

_____

_____

_____

_____

_____

Day 22

Great morning, God. Great morning, Jesus. Great morning, Holy Spirit. Thank you, God, for this day that you have made, and we are glad and rejoicing in it. Forgive us, God, for the things we have said, done, thought, and felt that are not pleasing to you nor lining up with your word.

Spirit of the living God, fall fresh on us today. Melt us, mold us, fill us, and use us for your glory. God, we are so thankful for every new day that you give us. We are thankful for every breath we take. Lord, we make ourselves available to you from the crown of our heads to the souls of our feet, to be used however you see fit.

This day we decree and declare that the blessings of the Lord shall make us rich in every area of our lives while adding no sorrow. Deliver us and send increase in our spirits, bodies, and finances. Thank you for revelation according to your word in John 8:35-43: *"And the servant abideth not in the house for ever: but the Son abideth ever. If the Son therefore shall make you free, ye shall be free indeed. I know that ye are Abraham's seed; but ye seek to kill me, because my word hath no place in you. I speak that which I have seen with my Father: and ye do that which ye have seen with your father. They answered and said unto him, Abraham is our father. Jesus saith unto them, If ye were*

Abraham's children, ye would do the works of Abraham. But now ye seek to kill me, a man that hath told you the truth, which I have heard of God: this did not Abraham. Ye do the deeds of your father. Then said they to him, We be not born of fornication; we have one Father, even God. Jesus said unto them, If God were your Father, ye would love me: for I proceeded forth and came from God; neither came I of myself, but he sent me. Why do ye not understand my speech? Even because ye cannot hear my word."

Help us to emulate how you have shown compassion and love to free others. There is power in forgiveness as we free ourselves from the bondage of holding on to the past. We make a choice today to forgive, love, worship, and pray so as to be in a proper posture before you. It is in the name of Jesus that we do pray. Amen.

Stimulating Thought

Studies have shown that worry and stress can make people sick, eventually leading to death over an extended period of time. As a body of believers, we often say that "prayer works" or "prayer makes a difference" in situations. Put it to action concerning all things in your life and look for the results of what you have prayed about. Make sure your heart is pure and your hands are clean and free of contaminants that would try to keep you from gaining all that God has for you. He came that you might have an abundant life.

Reflections

_____

_____

_____

_____

Day 23

Great morning, God. Great morning, Jesus. Great morning, Holy Spirit. Thank you, God, for this day that you have made, and we are glad and rejoicing in it. Forgive us, God, for the things we have said, done, thought, and felt that are not pleasing to you nor lining up with your word.

God, give us power, wisdom, love, and peace. Our desire is to walk in a manner worthy of the call you have placed upon our lives. Increase our compassion for our fellow man, to reach out to lost souls with an effective witness. God, you see and know all things that take place with us, so let nothing remain in our thoughts, actions, or words that would bring shame to your name or destroy our witness. Thank you, God, for every soul mattering to you and for heaven rejoicing every time a sinner receives Christ Jesus.

We are thankful for the compassion you have shown us and still show us according to 1 Peter 4:1-8: *"Forasmuch then as Christ hath suffered for us in the flesh, arm yourselves likewise with the same mind: for he that hath suffered in the flesh hath ceased from sin; that he no longer should live the rest of his time in the flesh to the lusts of men, but to the will of God. For the time past of our life may suffice us to have wrought the will of the Gentiles, when we walked in lasciviousness, lusts, excess of wine, revellings, banquetings, and abominable idolatries: wherein they think it strange that ye run not with them to the same excess of riot, speaking evil of you: who shall give account to him that is ready to judge the quick and the dead. For this cause was the gospel preached also to them that are dead, that they might be judged according to men in the flesh, but live according to God in the spirit. But the end of all things is at hand: be ye therefore sober, and watch unto prayer. And above all things have fervent charity among yourselves: for charity shall cover the multitude of sins."*

Teach us how to love ourselves and others even as you have loved us unconditionally. Thank you for the deliverance that comes when we can love and forgive ourselves and others. We are free to be who you have made us, not bound by the constraints of the past. This is a great day because you made it and we will expect greatness to come from it. It is in the name of Jesus that we pray. Amen.

Stimulating Thought

What's on your mind? What are you thinking? The words that come from your mouth are a reflection of what is in your heart and mind. Are you feeding your spirit something with substance that will stick with you, or are you constantly consuming junk from the news, sitcoms, inappropriate jokes, social media blurbs, or conversations that tear down and contaminate others? Monitor your diet by reading and/or listening to the word, inspirational materials, and positive literature and videos to build up and edify your spirit to be fit. The word tells us, *"whatsoever things are true, whatsoever things are honest, whatsoever things are just, whatsoever things are pure, whatsoever things are lovely, whatsoever things are of good report; if there be any virtue, and if there be any praise,* **think on these things"** (Philippians 4:8, my emphasis).

Reflections

_____

_____

_____

_____

_____

_____

_____

Day 24

Great morning, God. Great morning, Jesus. Great morning, Holy Spirit. Thank you, God, for this day that you have made, and we are glad and rejoicing in it. Forgive us, God, for the things we have said, done, thought, and felt that are not pleasing to you nor lining up with your word.

We give you glory today in all that we do as unto you, Lord. Without you we could do nothing but fail. Your way, O Lord, and your will be done in our lives. Keep us on the paths of righteousness so that we may enter into all that you have planned for us. Matthew 7:13-14 directs us: *"Enter ye in at the strait gate: for wide is the gate, and broad is the way, that leadeth to destruction, and many there be which go in thereat: because strait is the gate, and narrow is the way, which leadeth unto life, and few there be that find it."*

We desire to be counted among the few that find the way you have mapped out for a rewarding end. So let the mind of Christ be in us today when we make choices that will not only affect us but those around us as well. Opportunities are available and waiting for us to take, so give us the courage to take them by stepping outside of what has been comfortable. Remove distractions and keep our eyes focused on the prize as we seek to meet every deadline. In Jesus's name we pray. Amen.

Stimulating Thought

How are you presenting yourself to God and the world? We are vessels that God was proud to create, for we know he said we are good. If we are good in his sight, we must present ourselves as living sacrifices to God. He sees and knows everything about us anyway. Aside from what God sees, we should be concerned with what we are showing people around us from day to day. As you represent God and reflect him, can people see that? Be mindful of words released and actions taken. Set the example for a high standard of living by displaying the fruit of the Spirit in your life instead of being made an example of how not to live because of the corruption and confusion following after you.

Reflections

_____

_____

_____

_____

_____

_____

_____

Day 25

Great morning, God. Great morning, Jesus. Great morning, Holy Spirit. Thank you, God, for this day that you have made, and we are glad and rejoicing in it. Forgive us, God, for the things we have said, done, thought, and felt that are not pleasing to you nor lining up with your word.

We are in awe of you this morning, God, as our hearts cry out for more of you. Thank you for every place that you bring us to in life and for the reasons you allow us each experience. Give us the strength and endurance to go through rejoicing and to pass the test every time.

We honor your word according to Ephesians 1:3-14: *"Blessed be the God and Father of our Lord Jesus Christ, who hath blessed us with all spiritual blessings in heavenly places in Christ: according as he hath chosen us in him before the foundation of the world, that we should be holy and without blame before him in love: having predestinated us unto the adoption of children by Jesus Christ to himself, according to the good pleasure of his will, to the praise of the glory of his grace, wherein he hath made us accepted in the beloved. In whom we have redemption through his blood, the forgiveness of sins, according to the riches of his grace; wherein he hath abounded toward us in all wisdom and prudence;*

having made known unto us the mystery of his will, according to his good pleasure which he hath purposed in himself: that in the dispensation of the fulness of times he might gather together in one all things in Christ, both which are in heaven, and which are on earth; even in him: in whom also we have obtained an inheritance, being predestinated according to the purpose of him who worketh all things after the counsel of his own will: that we should be to the praise of his glory, who first trusted in Christ. In whom ye also trusted, after that ye heard the word of truth, the gospel of your salvation: in whom also after that ye believed, ye were sealed with that holy Spirit of promise, which is the earnest of our inheritance until the redemption of the purchased possession, unto the praise of his glory."

God, no matter what state we may find ourselves in, you always bring us back to where we need to be when we open our hearts and spirits to allow you to do a work in us. Father God, we give you glory and bless your name today and forevermore. It is in the name of Jesus that we do pray. Amen.

Stimulating Thought

Do you sometimes look around at the lives of others who appear to be doing things outside of the will of God but seem to get away with it? It is part of human nature to feel like the wicked get away with things because they seem to be thriving, prospering, and getting ahead in life. Well, the truth of the matter is: they are not. The word of God tells us that he chastens those whom he loves. Therefore, God is dealing with everyone for any actions that go against his word and will. And God does things in a manner that will not expose us or make us look bad, but he has a way that is mighty sweet to get our attention and to set us back on the right path when we are doing wrong. Know that God has all things under control and that he did not leave it up to us to set everything right. He is not concerned about our opinion, just our obedience to love and treat others right. A wise person said that God once spoke, "No one is right but me." That is profound because God is indeed the only one who is right. We simply carry out the purpose and plan he has laid out for our lives.

Reflections

_____

_____

_____

_____

_____

_____

_____

Day 26

Great morning, God. Great morning, Jesus. Great morning, Holy Spirit. Thank you, God, for this day that you have made, and we are glad and rejoicing in it. Forgive us, God, for the things we have said, done, thought, and felt that are not pleasing to you nor lining up with your word.

Thank you this morning for the joy and gladness on the inside, for you touched us to rise from our rest. Each day our hearts still cry for more of you. Fill us with your Holy Spirit so that everything coming from us will leave a lasting impression of the presence of the Lord.

Endue us with your presence until your power shakes the very foundation of what the enemy has tried to build up. Thank you for your word according to Ephesians 2:14-22 (GNT): *"For Christ himself has brought us peace by making Jews and Gentiles one people. With his own body he broke down the wall that separated them and kept them enemies. He abolished the Jewish Law with its commandments and rules, in order to create out of the two races one new people in union with himself, in this way making peace. By his death on the cross Christ destroyed their enmity; by means of the cross he united both races into one body and brought them back to God. So Christ came and preached the Good News of peace to all—to you Gentiles, who were far away from God, and to the Jews, who were near to him. It is through Christ that all of us, Jews and Gentiles, are able to come in the one Spirit into the presence of the Father. So then, you Gentiles are not foreigners or strangers any longer; you are now citizens together with God's people and members of the family of God. You, too, are built upon the foundation laid by the apostles and prophets, the cornerstone being Christ Jesus himself. He is the one who holds the whole building together and makes it grow into a sacred temple dedicated to the Lord. In union with him you too are being built together with all the others into a place where God lives through his Spirit."*

You have shown us many great things that come from the power of oneness. Thank you for making this nation cohesive as one again. Let one voice come from the body of Christ as we all speak the same message: the kingdom of God. Give us a genuine love for one another as we love you. It is in the name of Jesus we pray. Amen.

Stimulating Thought

Have you ever asked someone for assistance in a situation? Were you given an answer to help you but it wasn't the one you desired, so you rejected it? Each day we ask God questions and he always answers us. Do we accept what he says or what he allows? Part of our growth is being willing to accept something new. Sometimes we already have our minds made up about the answer we expect in a situation, but is that the best option for our lives? Just imagine how much further we could be in life if we would be open to hearing and obeying the voice of God.

Reflections

_____

_____

_____

_____

_____

_____

_____

Day 27

Great morning, God. Great morning, Jesus. Great morning, Holy Spirit. Thank you, God, for this day that you have made, and we are glad and rejoicing in it. Forgive us, God, for the things we have said, done, thought, and felt that are not pleasing to you nor lining up with your word.

Thank you for the joy of the Lord being our strength today. God, we come asking for wisdom today in all that we say, do, and think. Let us not move in our own strength and knowledge, but rather build up our trust in you to follow your direction in all things. You have freed us from sin, poverty, fear, oppression, and depression through your word and the blood of Jesus. Give us the boldness to fully walk in what you have given us to use.

Develop and stretch us in the necessary areas of our lives so that we can be effective in impacting the kingdom. Thank you for your word according to 2 Peter 3:8-14: *"But, beloved, be not ignorant of this one thing, that one day is with the Lord as a thousand years, and a thousand years as one day. The Lord is not slack concerning his promise, as some men count slackness; but is longsuffering to us-ward, not willing that any should perish, but that all should come to repentance. But the day of the Lord will come as a thief in the night; in the which the heavens shall pass away with a great noise, and the elements shall melt with fervent heat, the earth also and the works that are therein shall be burned up. Seeing then that all these things shall be dissolved, what manner of persons ought ye to be in all holy conversation and godliness, looking for and hasting unto the coming of the day of God, wherein the heavens being on fire shall be dissolved, and the elements shall melt with fervent heat? Nevertheless we, according to his promise, look for new heavens and a new earth, wherein dwelleth righteousness. Wherefore, beloved, seeing that ye look for such things, be diligent that ye may be found of him in peace, without spot, and blameless."*

Keep our eyes focused on the prize as we remain diligent about our Father's business. Let us not grow weary in doing good so that we will not faint but continue to press on. God, you have been so gracious to us that quitting on this journey is not an option, because you provide all the tools necessary for us to achieve victory. It is in the name of Jesus that we pray. Amen.

Stimulating Thought

Each day that you accomplish goals, do you give credit to God? The things we do are not by our own might but by his Spirit who dwells in us. Tell God "Thank you" for the little things in life. He wants you to have a blessed and happy life in all things that are taking place. When we can be thankful where we are, he will allow us to go beyond.

Reflections

_____

_____

_____

_____

Day 28

Great morning, God. Great morning, Jesus. Great morning, Holy Spirit. Thank you, God, for this day that you have made, and we are glad and rejoicing in it. Forgive us, God, for the things we have said, done, thought, and felt that are not pleasing to you nor lining up with your word.

Teach us, O Lord, in the areas we need to be taught. Heal our hearts from every hurt and disappointment. Dismiss all thoughts that rise to give us an excuse for why we are not where we think we should be in life, and help us accept responsibility for our own choices and actions.

Purge us, Lord, of all the frustration that comes as a result of miscalculated plans and preparation for life. Let the word according to Ephesians 4:17-32 take root in us: *"This I say therefore, and testify in the Lord, that ye henceforth walk not as other Gentiles walk, in the vanity of their mind, having the understanding darkened, being alienated from the life of God through the ignorance that is in them, because of the blindness of their heart: who being past feeling have given themselves over unto lasciviousness, to work all uncleanness with greediness. But ye have not so learned Christ; if so be that ye have heard him, and have been taught by him, as the truth is in Jesus: that ye put off concerning the former conversation the old man, which is corrupt according to the deceitful lusts; and be renewed in the spirit of your mind; and that ye put on the new man, which after God is created in righteousness and true holiness. Wherefore putting away lying, speak every man truth with his neighbor: for we are members one of another. Be ye angry, and sin not: let not the sun go down upon your wrath: neither give place to the devil. Let him that stole steal no more: but rather let him labour, working with his hands the thing which is good, that he may have to give to him that needeth. Let no corrupt communication proceed out of your mouth, but that which is good to the use of edifying, that it may minister grace unto the hearers. And grieve not the holy Spirit of God, whereby ye are sealed unto the day of redemption. Let all bitterness, and wrath, and anger, and clamour, and evil speaking, be put away from you, with all malice: and be ye kind one to another, tenderhearted, forgiving one another, even as God for Christ's sake hath forgiven you."*

Open our eyes of understanding and sharpen our discernment to recognize what spirits are operating in our mist. We bind any backlash the enemy attempts to bring against us for being obedient to your instructions, God. We yield and trust you no matter what, God. Arise, God, and scatter our enemies. We thank you in advance for results today in response to our prayers. In Jesus's name we do pray. Amen.

Stimulating Thought

Have you taken time lately to thank God for his Holy Spirit? What would life be like without the presence of the Holy Spirit? We might not conduct our lives to go in the right direction with the choices and decisions we make. Possibly we would not even operate in the fruit of the Spirit. That is a scary thought: people walking around, acting and treating one another any kind of way—not just some of the time but all the time. Without the Holy Spirit we would not have comfort and peace as we do now. The main attribute that most of us relate to the Holy Spirit is the power he brings. Can you imagine walking around through an entire lifetime with no power—like having no power in a home, with anything requiring power not working? That is the case when we reject the Holy Spirit or never receive him when he desires to reside in us. Open up and let him in today so that you will be built up and walk in the fullness of power that God has for each of us.

Reflections

_____

_____

_____

_____

_____

_____

_____

Day 29

Great morning, God. Great morning, Jesus. Great morning, Holy Spirit. Thank you, God, for this day that you have made, and we are glad and rejoicing in it. Forgive us, God, for the things we have said, done, thought, and felt that are not pleasing to you nor lining up with your word.

Thank you for who you are in our lives today and every day. Thank you for being our savior, helper, healer, provider, protector, comforter, and peace. Thank you for giving us dreams and visions. Manifest your glory as the vision comes to pass by the provisions you send to feed it.

Apply your word to our lives according to Ephesians 5:6-17 (NIV): *"Let no one deceive you with empty words, for because of such things God's wrath comes on those who are disobedient. Therefore do not be partners with them. For you were once darkness, but now you are light in the Lord. Live as children of light (for the fruit of the light consists in all goodness, righteousness and truth) and find out what pleases the Lord. Have nothing to do with the fruitless deeds of darkness, but rather expose them. It is shameful even to mention what the disobedient do in secret. But everything exposed by the light becomes visible—and everything that is illuminated becomes a light. This is why it is said: 'Wake up, sleeper, rise from the dead, and Christ will shine on you.' Be very careful, then, how you live—not as unwise but as wise, making the most of every opportunity, because the days are evil. Therefore do not be foolish, but understand what the Lord's will is."*

We thank you for the opportunities you present for us to grow so that we will appreciate the blessings as they arrive. From this day forward we are dismissing our disappointments because you have a greater plan in mind for us than what we have, and we expel all of the excuses we have hidden behind so we didn't have to perform at the level of potential you placed in us. God, you are great because you made us free even when you knew what we would do along the way. We rejoice in you and bless your name for what you are doing in the lives of people all around the world. Thank you for the blessings in the lives of others. Thank you for miracles, signs, and wonders. In Jesus's name we pray. Amen.

Stimulating Thought

How well do you know yourself? God knows the very hairs upon each of our heads and the structure of our DNA. Take time to get to know yourself instead of who you want people to know. We go through life trying to be who we think we should be because of the standards society has set. Go before our heavenly Father and ask him who you really are and what you should be. He is the author and finisher of our faith, the writer of the script for our lives. As you get to know him better, you find out more about yourself. Going deeper in God reveals more about our lives because he will open up and expose things to us that no one else has access to. I dare you to ask God who you really are.

Reflections

Day 30

Great morning, God. Great morning, Jesus. Great morning, Holy Spirit. Thank you, God, for this day that you have made, and we are glad and rejoicing in it. Forgive us, God, for the things we have said, done, thought, and felt that are not pleasing to you nor lining up with your word.

Our souls cry "Hallelujah!" to you, Lord. We magnify and glorify you, Lord God. With humbled hearts, we come before your throne this morning, praying on behalf of souls all around the world. Save those who are lost in every nation. Direct those wandering in the streets to the paths of righteousness. Turn hearts of stone to hearts of flesh. Bring together in agreement the spirits of those who are indifferent.

God, we realize that our thoughts and ways are not like yours, but help us to at least get things right so that we don't miss your plan for us. Give us a praying spirit to pray at all times about all things so that we don't incorrectly step into situations we don't need to face. Each day offers us so many benefits and blessings that we are grateful for. You give us the ability to breathe without machines. The blood flows through our bodies to all our limbs. Thank you, God, for all these provisions while we still have the ability to give you thanks. Your word reminds us of what Jesus has already done in us according to Luke 9:1-11: *"Then he called his twelve disciples together, and gave them power and authority over all devils, and to cure diseases. And he sent them to preach the kingdom of God, and to heal the sick. And he said unto them, Take nothing for your journey, neither staves, nor scrip, neither bread, neither money; neither have two coats apiece. And whatsoever house ye enter into, there abide, and thence depart. And whosoever will not receive you, when ye go out of that city, shake off the very dust from your feet for a testimony against them. And they departed, and went through the towns, preaching the gospel, and healing every where. Now Herod the tetrarch heard of all that was done by him: and he was perplexed, because that it was said of some, that John was risen from the dead; and of some, that Elias had appeared; and of others, that one of the old prophets was risen again. And Herod said, John have I beheaded: but who is this, of whom I hear such things? And he desired to see him. And the apostles, when they were returned, told him all that they had done. And he took them, and went aside privately into a desert place belonging to the city called Bethsaida. And the people, when they knew it, followed him: and he received them, and spake unto them of the kingdom of God, and healed them that had need of healing."*

Increase our courage and boldness to operate in the power and authority you have given us to heal the sick and raise the dead. Let miracles, signs, and wonders follow us because we believe. We are looking for greater things to happen in this new approaching season. It is in the name of Jesus we do pray. Amen.

Stimulating Thought

Each day we look around at the amazing things that God does from the time he wakes us up until we lie down to rest. He allows the sun to rise and set. The temperature is adjusted sometimes within minutes. Then we see a beautiful display of art through nature. If God can do this every day, how much more can he do through each of us when we yield to him! Let God use you to do great things, because he has need of you. Don't ever feel like you are useless and can't offer anything. God simply wants you to come as a willing vessel, just as you are. After all, he created you and placed everything in you that is needed. Be confident in God today and in who he created you to be.

Reflections

_____

_____

_____

_____

_____

_____

_____

Day 31

Great morning, God. Great morning, Jesus. Great morning, Holy Spirit. Thank you, God, for this day that you have made, and we are glad and rejoicing in it. Forgive us, God, for the things we have said, done, thought, and felt that are not pleasing to you nor lining up with your word.

We give you glory, God, for all that you have done and for everything that will take place. Your grace is sufficient for our lives each day. Nothing that happens is by accident and you never make a mistake in what you allow. We embrace every second of our lives and the opportunities to grow as they are presented to us.

Your word is an affirmation according to 2 Corinthians 4:1-11 (NIV): *"Therefore, since through God's mercy we have this ministry, we do not lose heart. Rather, we have renounced secret and shameful ways; we do not use deception, nor do we distort the word of God. On the contrary, by setting forth the truth plainly we commend ourselves to everyone's conscience in the sight of God. And even if our gospel is veiled, it is veiled to those who are perishing. The god of this age has blinded the minds of unbelievers, so that they cannot see the light of the gospel that displays the glory of Christ, who is the image of God. For what we preach is not ourselves, but Jesus Christ as Lord, and ourselves as your servants for Jesus' sake. For God, who said, 'Let light shine out of darkness,' made his light shine in our hearts to give us the light of the knowledge of God's glory displayed in the face of Christ. But we have this treasure in jars of clay to show that this all-surpassing power is from God and not from us. We are hard pressed on every side, but not crushed; perplexed, but not in despair; persecuted, but not abandoned; struck down, but not destroyed. We always carry around in our body the death of Jesus, so that the life of Jesus may also be revealed in our body. For we who are alive are always being given over to death for Jesus' sake, so that his life may also be revealed in our mortal body."*

Thank you for showing us our worth to you. Make us a good return on your investment through the lives that we live. We want to make you smile, God, as you look upon us each day. As we praise and worship you with sincere hearts, let the sweet fragrance of our adoration reach your nostrils. Come and dwell in our praise as we invoke your presence. We receive all that you have in store for our spirits this day as you pour into us. It is in the name of Jesus that we do pray. Amen.

Stimulating Thought

Do you feel thirsty some days, as if nothing quenches or satisfies the longing inside you? Jesus said that he would give living water to those desiring it and that they would never thirst again. With the rich supply of this water available to us, why are we still thirsty? Perhaps we are not drinking the water properly or maybe we don't want to stop engaging in other activities long enough to taste and see that this water is really good. Whatever the case, the well is available, ready to be primed for the water to come flowing out. After drinking from this source, the faucets inside of us begin to flow like rivers of living water waiting to be released. Get your word and drink until your soul is satisfied, because the supply never runs out. There is enough to take care of the entire world, so don't hold back in drinking this living water.

Reflections

_____

_____

_____

_____

_____

_____

_____

Day 32

Great morning, God. Great morning, Jesus. Great morning, Holy Spirit. Thank you, God, for this day that you have made, and we are glad and rejoicing in it. Forgive us, God, for the things we have said, done, thought, and felt that are not pleasing to you nor lining up with your word.

We set our minds on things that are lovely, pure, and of good report this morning. You are our God and we are your people. Keep us focused and on task today, because we know that many distractions will come and try to snatch the word and get us off balance. Make this day a productive one as we do all things unto you, Lord.

Thank you, God, for relieving us from tension and stress today, for it is not your desire for us to be anxious. Deliver all who face panic attacks to no longer be gripped by fear in those situations. Hebrews 6:9-18 (NIV) shares, *"Even though we speak like this, dear friends, we are convinced of better things in your case—the things that have to do with salvation. God is not unjust; he will not forget your work and the love you have shown him as you have helped his people and continue to help them. We want each of you to show this same diligence to the very end, so that what you hope for may be fully realized. We do not want you to become lazy, but to imitate those who through faith and patience inherit what has been promised. When God made his promise to Abraham, since there was no one greater for him to swear by, he swore by himself, saying, 'I will surely bless you and give you many descendants.' And so after waiting patiently, Abraham received what was promised. People swear by someone greater than themselves, and the oath confirms what is said and puts an end to all argument. Because God wanted to make the unchanging nature of his purpose very clear to the heirs of what was promised, he confirmed it with an oath. God did this so that, by two unchangeable things in which it is impossible for God to lie, we who have fled to take hold of the hope set before us may be greatly encouraged."*

Put our lives in perspective as we consider what you have done and continue to do each day on our behalf. We rejoice in you, God, for working all things out for our good. Even when things don't always look good to our natural eyes, we know that you have it all under control. Our hope is built on our trust in Jesus Christ because whatever we ask in his name shall be done. In Jesus's name we do pray this prayer. Amen.

Stimulating Thought

Some days feel harder than others but the Lord is still with us every step of the way. When we stop to think about what seem to be challenges in our lives, are they really that hard in the grand scheme of things? After all, Jesus hung nailed to a cross for hours after being whipped, and he did not complain or come down to save himself. He decided to stay there to suffer for every one of us. With that said, if he did that for us, knowing that we would still fall from time to time, can we really say life is that rough? We don't have to give our lives as a sacrifice for anyone else. Anytime we call on our heavenly Father, he answers. When you feel like you have it bad and are going through something horrible, stop to count your many blessings to determine if your blessings outweigh your problems.

Reflections

_____

_____

_____

_____

_____

_____

_____

Day 33

Great morning, God. Great morning, Jesus. Great morning, Holy Spirit. Thank you, God, for this day that you have made, and we are glad and rejoicing in it. Forgive us, God, for the things we have said, done, thought, and felt that are not pleasing to you nor lining up with your word.

Arise, God, and scatter every enemy. The earth and everything within it belong to you, so we are thankful. Your way, O Lord, and your will be done this day. Give us a praying spirit to pray for one another. Prayer makes a difference in all our lives when we utilize this tool you have given to us.

We meditate on your word today according to 1 Timothy 2:1-6: *"I exhort therefore, that, first of all, supplications, prayers, intercessions, and giving of thanks, be made for all men; for kings, and for all that are in authority; that we may lead a quiet and peaceable life in all godliness and honesty. For this is good and acceptable in the sight of God our Saviour; who will have all men to be saved, and to come unto the knowledge of the truth. For there is one God, and one mediator between God and men, the man Christ Jesus; who gave himself a ransom for all, to be testified in due time."*

Thank you for Christ being our righteous leader by the example he set for all mankind. We lift up the prayer shield on behalf of leaders today in the body of Christ and in our nation. Thank you for results that will please you, God. Thank you for the grace upon their lives to lead your people. Let love fill our hearts to come together as one to accomplish the great things you have in store for us. It is in the name of Jesus that we do pray. Amen.

Stimulating Thought

Are you in position to receive blessings for your life? God has something in store for every one of us, but we must be in the right place when that time comes. Sometimes we get busy with our plans for life and move out of the place we need to be to fulfill God's plan. We often hear the cliché to "stay in your lane," but it really has a greater meaning than simply avoiding anything that you are not equipped to do. When you are covering roles not intended for you, you will be out of place and preoccupied when it is time to be blessed. Be content with what God has given you to do and wait on the blessing he has for you.

Reflections

_____

_____

_____

_____

_____

_____

_____

Day 34

Great morning, God. Great morning, Jesus. Great morning, Holy Spirit. Thank you, God, for this day that you have made, and we are glad and rejoicing in it. Forgive us, God, for the things we have said, done, thought, and felt that are not pleasing to you nor lining up with your word.

We receive and thank you for your love today, Lord. You love us more than we love ourselves and one another. Keep our minds focused on you today, not on our situations, circumstances, or emotions.

Let us be busy about the work set before us today to share the good news with the many souls we come in contact with. Divine assignments have been given for the people we shall meet, so prepare our hearts and theirs. Guide us according to your word in 2 Peter 1:1-12 (NLT): *"This letter is from Simon Peter, a slave and apostle of Jesus Christ. I am writing to you who share the same precious faith we have. This faith was given to you because of the justice and fairness of Jesus Christ, our God and Savior. May God give you more and more grace and peace as you grow in your knowledge of God and Jesus our Lord. By his divine power, God has given us everything we need for living a godly life. We have received all of this by coming to know him, the one who called us to himself by means of his marvelous glory and excellence. And because of his glory and excellence, he has given us great and precious promises. These are the promises that enable you to share his divine nature and escape the world's corruption caused by human desires. In view of all this, make every effort to respond to God's promises. Supplement your faith with a generous provision of moral excellence, and moral excellence with knowledge, and knowledge with self-control, and self-control with patient endurance, and patient endurance with godliness, and godliness with brotherly affection, and brotherly affection with love for everyone. The more you grow like this, the more productive and useful you will be in your knowledge of our Lord Jesus Christ. But those who fail to develop in this way are shortsighted or blind, forgetting that they have been cleansed from their old sins. So, dear brothers and sisters, work hard to prove that you really are among those God has called and chosen. Do these things, and you will never fall away. Then God will give you a grand entrance into the eternal Kingdom of our Lord and Savior Jesus Christ. Therefore, I will always remind you about these things— even though you already know them and are standing firm in the truth you have been taught."*

God, keep us true to your word, not deviating from a life that lines up with your word and pleases you. As we live in obedience to you, God, we see the results of good fruit being produced. Let this fruit remain for generations to come. Dissolve all feelings of discord and chaos so that we may display your character through brotherly and sisterly love. We are excited about your unfailing love that we experience every second of each day as you continue to release oxygen into the atmosphere and as the blood of Jesus still covers us. It is in the name of Jesus that we do pray. Amen.

Stimulating Thought

Do you feel like you always have balance in your life? God wants us to be well balanced in our bodies, minds, and souls, not overwhelmed. For that balance to be in place and manifest in our lives, we must do something. Take time a few minutes each day to read the word, inspirational writings, and other material that brings you peace. Also spend time praying and communicating with God. Improve your life of worship each day as you go deeper with God. The more of him we have in us, the greater the balance we have among the various components of our lives.

Reflections

Day 35

Great morning, God. Great morning, Jesus. Great morning, Holy Spirit. Thank you, God, for this day that you have made, and we are glad and rejoicing in it. Forgive us, God, for the things we have said, done, thought, and felt that are not pleasing to you nor lining up with your word.

You are our peace in the midst of all the chaos and confusion taking place around us. No matter how unstable conditions become in the world, you always remain constant, God. You reign over the billions of people in all the earth. There is none like you, God. No one can do what you do because you are God alone.

Transform our temperament to reflect your dwelling in us. Thank you for the reminder according to your word in Matthew 9:4-13: *"And Jesus knowing their thoughts said, Wherefore think ye evil in your hearts? For whether is easier, to say, Thy sins be forgiven thee; or to say, Arise, and walk? But that ye may know that the Son of man hath power on earth to forgive sins, (then saith he to the sick of the palsy,) Arise, take up thy bed, and go unto thine house. And he arose, and departed to his house. But when the multitudes saw it, they marvelled, and glorified God, which had given such power unto men. And as Jesus passed forth from thence, he saw a man, named Matthew, sitting at the*

receipt of custom: and he saith unto him, Follow me. And he arose, and
followed him. And it came to pass, as Jesus sat at meat in the house,
behold, many publicans and sinners came and sat down with him and
his disciples. And when the Pharisees saw it, they said unto his disciples,
Why eateth your Master with publicans and sinners? But when Jesus
heard that, he said unto them, They that be whole need not a physician,
but they that are sick. But go ye and learn what that meaneth, I will
have mercy, and not sacrifice: for I am not come to call the righteous, but
sinners to repentance."

Thank you for being the only righteous judge over all things that take place in the earth, God. You do all things with a purpose, and we must accept your plan. You see the end of a thing before it even begins, and we thank you for knowing the outcome. Expand our vision to see things outside of the small frame we tend to see things within. Thank you for the BIGGER plan and picture you have in mind for us. We trust you with whole hearts and will follow your lead, God. It is in the name of Jesus we do pray. Amen.

Stimulating Thought

Do you have some goals and dreams but are simply afraid to try? You may not know where to start or who to contact, but you can do it. Fear is only a *False Evidence Appearing Real* to you. Begin to speak to that fear and encourage yourself—because YOU CAN DO IT. It is amazing the things someone can accomplish once there is a mind-set to get it done. For some people, nervous energy inspires the completion of a project. With others, all things must be organized and planned precisely down to the very second and penny. Regardless of your method or your phobia, pray and ask God for help to get it done, because he will complete in you what he has begun. Disregard all negative conversations and thoughts, and think on only what is good and positive. You are good and well able to do all things through Christ who strengthens you.

Reflections

_____

_____

_____

_____

_____

_____

_____

Day 36

Great morning, God. Great morning, Jesus. Great morning, Holy Spirit. Thank you, God, for this day that you have made, and we are glad and rejoicing in it. Forgive us, God, for the things we have said, done, thought, and felt that are not pleasing to you nor lining up with your word.

Lord, we pray today for direction and guidance in all things that shall take place in our lives. We are convinced that you have a plan and purpose for all our lives even as that plan and purpose continue to unfold through the results we see manifesting every day. Thank you for being everywhere we go, present in all things that we do.

We appreciate the truth of your word according to Psalm 139:1-15: *"O lord, thou hast searched me, and known me. Thou knowest my downsitting and mine uprising, thou understandest my thought afar off. Thou compassest my path and my lying down, and art acquainted with all my ways. For there is not a word in my tongue, but, lo, O Lord, thou knowest it altogether. Thou hast beset me behind and before, and laid thine hand upon me. Such knowledge is too wonderful for me; it is high, I cannot attain unto it. Whither shall I go from thy spirit? or whither shall I flee from thy presence? If I ascend up into heaven, thou art there: if I make my bed in hell, behold, thou art there. If I take the wings of the morning, and dwell in the uttermost parts of the sea; even there shall thy hand lead me, and thy right hand shall hold me. If I say, Surely the darkness shall cover me; even the night shall be light about me. Yea, the darkness hideth not from thee; but the night shineth as the day: the darkness and the light are both alike to thee. For thou hast possessed my reins: thou hast covered me in my mother's womb. I will praise thee; for I am fearfully and wonderfully made: marvellous are thy works; and that my soul knoweth right well. My substance was not hid from thee, when I was made in secret, and curiously wrought in the lowest parts of the earth."*

Turn the mirror on us to show us the things you see in us that need improvement. Help us to accept the truth of what you reveal and to admit that we need to change. You are well able to deliver us fully in all the areas of life that seem hidden from others but not from you, God. You still love us in spite of what you see. Give us that level of love and compassion for one another so that we can make an even greater impact in the kingdom as your ambassadors. In Jesus's name we pray. Amen.

Stimulating Thought

It's time to tap into the greatness that is within you. We are all created in the image and likeness of God. He said from the beginning that everything he created is good. He never said we would not make mistakes, but he did say we are good. Be confident in the fact that greater is the God who is within you than the evil one in this world. Ask yourself, "Why would God place something so great in me if he didn't intend for me to use it?" Exactly. The potential, power, and ability have been resting in you from the time you were created, so take action to do something with them. Get excited about the life you have and the limitless possibilities. Rejoice when you see others around you moving in what they have been destined to do and then they will do the same for you. There is enough greatness in each of us to make the world an awesome place for everyone.

Reflections

_____

_____

_____

_____

_____

_____

_____

Day 37

Great morning, God. Great morning, Jesus. Great morning, Holy Spirit. Thank you, God, for this day that you have made, and we are glad and rejoicing in it. Forgive us, God, for the things we have said, done, thought, and felt that are not pleasing to you nor lining up with your word.

As we come before you in prayer this morning, God, we welcome your presence in us—the Holy Spirit. Give us a praying spirit as we engage your Holy Spirit to pray when we know not what to pray. Send the winds of change to blow away all chaos, confusion, and discord. Build us up in our faith and keep our minds sane, for you have said that you have not given us a spirit of fear, but of power, love, and a sound mind. We bind every satanic attack that comes against the minds of people and suggests any kind of mental illness or thoughts of suicide.

Your word confirms the value you place on our lives, for you sent Jesus with the purpose as revealed in John 10:1-18: *"Verily, verily, I say unto you, He that entereth not by the door into the sheepfold, but climbeth up some other way, the same is a thief and a robber. But he that entereth in by the door is the shepherd of the sheep. To him the porter openeth; and the sheep hear his voice: and he calleth his own sheep by name, and leadeth them out. And when he putteth forth his own sheep, he goeth before them, and the sheep follow him: for they know his voice. And a stranger will they not follow, but will flee from him: for they know not the voice of strangers. This parable spake Jesus unto them: but they understood not what things they were which he spake unto them. Then said Jesus unto them again, Verily, verily, I say unto you, I am the door of the sheep. All that ever came before me are thieves and robbers: but the sheep did not hear them. I am the door: by me if any man enter in, he shall be saved, and shall go in and out, and find pasture. The thief cometh not, but for to steal, and to kill, and to destroy: I am come that they might have life, and that they might have it more abundantly. I am the good shepherd: the good shepherd giveth his life for the sheep. But he that is an hireling, and not the shepherd, whose own the sheep are not, seeth the wolf coming, and leaveth the sheep, and fleeth: and the wolf catcheth them, and scattereth the sheep. The hireling fleeth, because he is an hireling, and careth not for the sheep. I am the good shepherd, and know my sheep, and am known of mine. As the Father knoweth me, even so know I the Father: and I lay down my life for the sheep. And other sheep I have, which are not of this fold: them also I must bring, and they shall hear my voice; and there shall be one fold, and one shepherd. Therefore doth my Father love me, because I lay down my life, that I might take it again. No man taketh it from me, but I lay it down of myself. I have power to lay it down, and I have power to take it again. This commandment have I received of my Father."*

Because of your gracious gift of life, we do not have the right to take the life of another or end our own, Father God. We cast down every vain imagination as we tune our ears to the voice of our Shepherd. Reveal every false shepherd and hireling through the discernment of the Holy Spirit. We decree and declare that we are whole because of the power in the blood of Jesus. Thank you for keeping us grounded and rooted in your word. It is in the name of Jesus that we do pray. Amen.

Stimulating Thought

As you advance forward to carry out your assignments for this day or week or month, stop to evaluate what things God has allowed you to accomplish in recent times. He gave you a vision to be carried out and provided what was needed. Did you do it? If not, no worries, because we serve a forgiving God. Ask God to redeem the time and give you the strategy and strength to finish. Distractions will come but we must make up our minds not to allow them to paralyze us. Nothing happens without God allowing it. Trials don't come to break us but to make us stronger, because he knows what we can bear. Everything in us is what he put in us. Don't throw in the towel and quit. You have time to get the job done. Pull up your bootstraps, dig in your heels, and just do it. We have God's Holy Spirit to help us.

Reflections

_____

_____

_____

_____

_____

_____

_____

Day 38

Great morning, God. Great morning, Jesus. Great morning, Holy Spirit. Thank you, God, for this day that you have made, and we are glad and rejoicing in it. Forgive us, God, for the things we have said, done, thought, and felt that are not pleasing to you nor lining up with your word.

Today we simply come with thankful hearts and humble spirits. You are so good to us and have everlasting mercy. Thank you for being the God who see and knows all things about us. Thank you for being the God who provides all that we need. Thank you for unmerited favor, even when we have not done all that we are supposed to do.

Lord, you are all-wise and all-knowing, revealing every answer we need at the right time. We accept your answers according to your word in Proverbs 16:1-13 (NLT): *"We can make our own plans, but the Lord gives the right answer. People may be pure in their own eyes, but the Lord examines their motives. Commit your actions to the Lord, and your plans will succeed. The Lord has made everything for his own purposes, even the wicked for a day of disaster. The Lord detests the proud; they will surely be punished. Unfailing love and faithfulness make atonement for sin. By fearing the Lord, people avoid evil. When people's lives please the Lord, even their enemies are at peace with them. Better to have little, with godliness, than to be rich and dishonest. We can make our plans, but the Lord determines our steps. The king speaks with divine wisdom; he must never judge unfairly. The Lord demands accurate scales and balances; he sets the standards for fairness. A king detests wrongdoing, for his rule is built on justice. The king is pleased with words from righteous lips; he loves those who speak honestly."*

God, your answer is never wrong, and we thank you for always being right. We dedicate our services to you in all that we do. It is because of you that we have life, health, and strength to get all things done. Let the wisdom that you have placed in us come forth when we speak, rather than the foolishness from any thoughts we entertain. The atmosphere is shifting as we begin to see a transfer of the things that the wicked possessed coming into the hands of the righteous. It is in the name of Jesus that we do pray. Amen.

Stimulating Thought

We all know that no one is perfect but God. Yet we struggle with asking for help as if it is a sin to need assistance. Pride goes before destruction, so kill it, sever it, and destroy it from your life if it has risen. You don't have to go through struggles all alone. God said ask and it shall be given to you. Ask God whom to go to or where to go for help. He will answer. Your answer may even be a matter of going to the word, where he has already directed us to go. Be sensitive to his Holy Spirit as he speaks.

Reflections

_____

_____

_____

_____

_____

_____

_____

_____

Day 39

Great morning, God. Great morning, Jesus. Great morning, Holy Spirit. Thank you, God, for this day that you have made, and we are glad and rejoicing in it. Forgive us, God, for the things we have said, done, thought, and felt that are not pleasing to you nor lining up with your word.

We lift our eyes to the hills where our help comes from, Lord. You are the joy and strength of our lives. God, you make all things possible for us and we thank you. Set a watch over our mouths, minds, and hearts today for nothing to come from us that you are not pleased with. Unify us in the body of Christ as denominational barriers are destroyed for us to be in one accord. We worship you in spirit and in truth.

Direct us on the best paths for our lives. Let the word according to Proverbs 15:24-33 (NLT) marinate in our spirits: *"The path of life leads upward for the wise; they leave the grave behind. The Lord tears down the house of the proud, but he protects the property of widows. The Lord detests evil plans, but he delights in pure words. Greed brings grief to the whole family, but those who hate bribes will live. The heart of the godly thinks carefully before speaking; the mouth of the wicked overflows with evil words. The Lord is far from the wicked, but he hears the prayers of the righteous. A cheerful look brings joy to the heart; good news makes for good health. If you listen to constructive criticism, you will be at home among the wise. If you reject discipline, you only harm yourself; but if you listen to correction, you grow in understanding. Fear of the Lord teaches wisdom; humility precedes honor."*

God, show us ourselves to see what you see and what others perceive about us. Thank you for privately correcting us and publicly rewarding us when we turn troublesome issues around. Build up our character and strengthen our integrity to leave nothing to question about how we live our lives for you from day to day. Look upon every leader in the land to be the first partakers and followers of the systems they implement and enforce. Give us obedient hearts to follow the leadership you have place us under. It is in the name of Jesus we pray. Amen.

Stimulating Thought

As we go through our lives, do we always take responsibility to own up to our faults? We serve a God who looks beyond our faults and sees the greater need in our lives. Take a moment to reflect each day and seek forgiveness for things done against God and others. It is much easier to say "I'm sorry" for a thing than to carry the load and let it build up within you more and more. Do not allow pride to overtake your life and keep you from reaching the places awaiting your arrival. Our actions can close the door to opportunities simply because we will not say "I'm sorry." Practice that phrase on those closest to you and see how good it feels to get those weights off your chest. It becomes easier over time and God appreciates the honesty.

Reflections

_____

_____

_____

_____

_____

_____

_____

Day 40

Great morning, God. Great morning, Jesus. Great morning, Holy Spirit. Thank you, God, for this day that you have made, and we are glad and rejoicing in it. Forgive us, God, for the things we have said, done, thought, and felt that are not pleasing to you nor lining up with your word.

We come to say "Thank you" for all that you have done and continue to do for us every day. You saved us when it seemed all hope was gone and the devil thought he had us. Your love lifted us out of the places we'd fallen into, and we thank you. Repair our hearts to set aside differences and come together with one another in love. Pull down the strongholds that have formed in the minds of people. God, you are still moving even now and it is time for your miracles to manifest.

Your word tells us according to Proverbs 18:4-20 (NLT): "*Wise words are like deep waters; wisdom flows from the wise like a bubbling brook. It is not right to acquit the guilty or deny justice to the innocent. Fools' words get them into constant quarrels; they are asking for a beating. The mouths of fools are their ruin; they trap themselves with their lips. Rumors are dainty morsels that sink deep into one's heart. A lazy person is as bad as someone who destroys things. The name of the*

Lord is a strong fortress; the godly run to him and are safe. The rich think of their wealth as a strong defense; they imagine it to be a high wall of safety. Haughtiness goes before destruction; humility precedes honor. Spouting off before listening to the facts is both shameful and foolish. The human spirit can endure a sick body, but who can bear a crushed spirit? Intelligent people are always ready to learn. Their ears are open for knowledge. Giving a gift can open doors; it gives access to important people! The first to speak in court sounds right—until the cross-examination begins. Flipping a coin can end arguments; it settles disputes between powerful opponents. An offended friend is harder to win back than a fortified city. Arguments separate friends like a gate locked with bars. Wise words satisfy like a good meal; the right words bring satisfaction."

Help us to choose our words wisely so that they will build up and encourage those who hear them. Keep our minds clear of all foolish thinking as we listen to only your voice for our day-to-day instructions. Purify our hearts to yield to and perform what you speak. It is in the name of Jesus that we pray. Amen.

Stimulating Thought

God rewards those who seek him. Spend less time looking for the praises of man and more time doing what will please God. God will never disappoint us, but people will fail us when we put our hope in them only. Where have you placed your hope? What kind of results are you receiving? Try trusting the all-wise and all-knowing God. He can and will take care of all your needs.

Reflections

_____

_____

Day 41

Great morning, God. Great morning, Jesus. Great morning, Holy Spirit. Thank you, God, for this day that you have made, and we are glad and rejoicing in it. Forgive us, God, for the things we have said, done, thought, and felt that are not pleasing to you nor lining up with your word.

Thank you for your splendor and majesty as you reign over all the earth, God. You are the creator of all the universe, and you know all things that exist and all that will take place. Lift our spirits today, for some are facing difficult times as loved ones have passed on and will not be present in their lives. Fill that void in the hearts of the many who are lonely or grieving. Turn the pain and sorrow around for healing and joy to come about. We know that you make no mistakes, and nothing is by accident. Your plan is best even when we do not understand it. Prepare our hearts to accept what you allow.

Strengthen every man, woman, boy, and girl today, for the enemy is seeking whom he may devour. The blood of Jesus covers every person today, and we speak life, healing, and protection to all. We agree with your word according to Psalm 138:1-8: *"I will praise thee with my whole heart: before the gods will I sing praise unto thee. I will worship toward thy holy temple, and praise thy name for thy lovingkindness and for thy truth: for thou hast magnified thy word above all thy name. In the day when I cried thou answeredst me, and strengthenedst me with strength in my soul. All the kings of the earth shall praise thee, O Lord, when they hear the words of thy mouth. Yea, they shall sing in the ways of the Lord: for great is the glory of the Lord. Though the Lord be high, yet hath he respect unto the lowly: but the proud he knoweth afar off. Though I walk in the midst of trouble, thou wilt revive me: thou shalt stretch forth thine hand against the wrath of mine enemies, and thy right hand shall save me. The Lord will perfect that which concerneth me: thy mercy, O Lord, endureth for ever: forsake not the works of thine own hands."*

Work miracles today that only you can perform so as to amaze the unbeliever until they come to know that you are the true and living God. Make ways today out of no way except by your power. Shield and protect in situations where man will not be able to explain what was done or how, but only that you, God, must have done it. Show yourself strong in lives today so that no question can be presented about who you are. For you are the I AM—Jehovah. We thank you for who you are and will be forevermore. In Jesus's name we pray. Amen.

Stimulating Thought

Have you ever faced tough situations in your life when you could not go to anyone except God? We all suffer afflictions in our lives, but God is always there with us to bring us out. He provides the way of escape, but it is up to us to take it. God gives us choices and waits for us to make one. His Holy Spirit guides us to make wise decisions, but sometimes our flesh ignores what he is saying. Then we want to blame God for our problems. When you find your back against a wall, pray immediately. Do not spend time toiling and stressing, because that will not change the situation. The sooner we go to God, the sooner we can receive the relief. Pray early, often, and honestly.

Reflections

_____

_____

_____

_____

_____

_____

_____

Day 42

Great morning, God. Great morning, Jesus. Great morning, Holy Spirit. Thank you, God, for this day that you have made, and we are glad and rejoicing in it. Forgive us, God, for the things we have said, done, thought, and felt that are not pleasing to you nor lining up with your word.

Our souls rejoice in knowing that you rule and reign over all the earth, heavenly Father. We magnify you, Lord. Today our spirits leap with great expectation for the great things you have done and will continue to do in the lives of your people. In areas where we lack confidence, inspire us to take action and do what you have placed in us to get done.

Grant us wisdom as we seek it from you, God. Thank you for your word concerning wisdom according to Proverbs 8:1-12: *"Doth not wisdom cry? and understanding put forth her voice? She standeth in the top of high places, by the way in the places of the paths. She crieth at the gates, at the entry of the city, at the coming in at the doors. Unto you, O men, I call; and my voice is to the sons of man. O ye simple, understand wisdom: and, ye fools, be ye of an understanding heart. Hear; for I will speak of excellent things; and the opening of my lips shall be right things. For my mouth shall speak truth; and wickedness is an abomination to my lips. All the words of my mouth are in righteousness; there is nothing froward or perverse in them. They are all plain to him that understandeth, and right to them that find knowledge. Receive my instruction, and not silver; and knowledge rather than choice gold. For wisdom is better than rubies; and all the things that may be desired are not to be compared to it. I wisdom dwell with prudence, and find out knowledge of witty inventions."*

As we walk in wisdom, enhance our lives to produce at an even higher level of excellence. Thank you for not leaving or forsaking us. Continue to be our source, peace, joy, and strength. Your word is immediate, so we decree now in the name of Jesus that we are the healed of the Lord walking in divine health. We are above, not beneath; we are the lender and no longer a borrower. Open doors that man tries to shut and give us the courage to walk through them. It is in the name of Jesus that we do pray. Amen.

Stimulating Thought

Every day is a day of thanksgiving when we think about God's goodness and mercy. It's not just one day a year that he blesses us and we should be thankful, but every day. New opportunities present themselves often, but fear rises and doubt creeps in, causing us not to redeem what is placed before us. Remind yourself that the blessings of the Lord make us rich and he adds no sorrow to them. He will not give you anything to bring you grief, but instead to maintain and enjoy. Tune in to what God is speaking for your life and accept what he allows. Silence the voice of every naysayer and connect with positive people.

Reflections

_____

_____

Day 43

Great morning, God. Great morning, Jesus. Great morning, Holy Spirit. Thank you, God, for this day that you have made, and we are glad and rejoicing in it. Forgive us, God, for the things we have said, done, thought, and felt that are not pleasing to you nor lining up with your word.

Let all that we do today bring pleasure to you, God. Renew our minds to think in a manner that lines up with your word and to take action to produce results. Clear any distorted vision so that we may see things as they really are, instead of some mirage or illusion as Satan might try to present to us. Tune our hearing to your voice and the sound from heaven.

Your word supersedes all things. We accept the word according to Psalm 89:15-19: *"Blessed is the people that know the joyful sound: they shall walk, O Lord, in the light of thy countenance. In thy name shall they rejoice all the day: and in thy righteousness shall they be exalted. For thou art the glory of their strength: and in thy favour our horn shall be exalted. For the Lord is our defence; and the Holy One of Israel is our king. Then thou spakest in vision to thy holy one, and saidst, I have laid help upon one that is mighty; I have exalted one chosen out of the people."*

Reveal to us the things you have chosen us for so that we will perform fully all that we are anointed to do. Strengthen and energize us to overcome every obstacle between us and the completion of our assignments. We have a great expectation for a positive day in every aspect. Our thoughts will stay on you and we yield to your Holy Spirit. It is in the name of Jesus we do pray. Amen.

Stimulating Thought

We run a hectic race some days on this journey called life. With that said, it is vital to pace yourself on the course of travel. Advance moderately, not going too fast to give out or too slow to make you feel like you will never make it. Make a list of what is needed to get to your destination. Prioritize what gets done first and how much time you spend on the various duties. When you feel overwhelmed, take a break and come back later. Set aside your pride and ask for help when needed. The results are remarkable when you enjoy your trip along the way.

Reflections

_____

_____

_____

_____

_____

_____

_____

Day 44

Great morning, God. Great morning, Jesus. Great morning, Holy Spirit. Thank you, God, for this day that you have made, and we are glad and rejoicing in it. Forgive us, God, for the things we have said, done, thought, and felt that are not pleasing to you nor lining up with your word.

God, you are faithful to your word and we thank you for that today. You have honored every promise you've made to us, not changing your mind or backing out on your word. We are blessed and highly favored in more ways than we can count. Keep complaints from coming out of our lips. Let praises continuously flow from us.

Thank you for the entire Bible that you have given us to apply to our lives. John 15:1-17 establishes our relationship with Christ, as it says: *"I am the true vine, and my Father is the husbandman. Every branch in me that beareth not fruit he taketh away: and every branch that beareth fruit, he purgeth it, that it may bring forth more fruit. Now ye are clean through the word which I have spoken unto you. Abide in me, and I in you. As the branch cannot bear fruit of itself, except it abide in the vine; no more can ye, except ye abide in me. I am the vine, ye are the branches: He that abideth in me, and I in him, the same bringeth forth much fruit: for without me ye can do nothing. If a man abide not in me, he is cast forth as a branch, and is withered; and men gather them, and cast them into the fire, and they are burned. If ye abide in me, and my words abide in you, ye shall ask what ye will, and it shall be done unto you. Herein is my Father glorified, that ye bear much fruit; so shall ye be my disciples. As the Father hath loved me, so have I loved you: continue ye in my love. If ye keep my commandments, ye shall abide in my love; even as I have kept my Father's commandments, and abide in his love. These things have I spoken unto you, that my joy might remain in you, and that your joy might be full. This is my commandment, That ye love one another, as I have loved you. Greater love hath no man than this, that a man lay down his life for his friends. Ye are my friends, if ye do whatsoever I command you. Henceforth I call you not servants; for the servant knoweth not what his lord doeth: but I have called you friends; for all things that I have heard of my Father I have made known unto you. Ye have not chosen me, but I have chosen you, and ordained you, that ye should go and bring forth fruit, and that your fruit should remain: that whatsoever ye shall ask of the Father in my name, he may give it you. These things I command you, that ye love one another."*

The love and friendship you have shown us, God, is flawless and we thank you. Help us to be a friend who shows agape love to every person. Love is the greatest gift you have given us and we thank you for it. We don't take you or your love for granted. Arise in us today to show your love like never before and to be an instrument of deliverance—beginning in our own lives as we practice loving ourselves. We are expecting great spiritual results as shadows of darkness get destroyed, no longer binding people. It is in the name of Jesus that we do pray. Amen.

Stimulating Thought

When you look in the mirror, are you pleased with all that you see? That is a loaded question because the mirror never lies but shows the truth. Many times, when we look in the natural mirror, we are not pleased with physical attributes that we have control over, like being overweight and in poor shape because of an unhealthy diet and lack of exercise, or looking tired from not getting enough sleep. What about when we look in the spiritual mirror, which is the word of God? Are we pleased with what we see there? Again, all these things we have control over because we make choices about how we will live. God makes available everything we need to be delivered from strongholds. It is up to us to receive it from him. He never forces anything on us like our parents did when they made us take medicine and vitamins each day because it was good for us. Make a decision about how you will look when you stand before the mirror, good or bad. Be happy with what you decide and do not complain.

Reflections

_____

_____

_____

_____

_____

_____

_____

Day 45

Great morning, God. Great morning, Jesus. Great morning, Holy Spirit. Thank you, God, for this day that you have made, and we are glad and rejoicing in it. Forgive us, God, for the things we have said, done, thought, and felt that are not pleasing to you nor lining up with your word.

We worship you in spirit and truth as we come before your throne this morning. Speak to our hearts, Holy Spirit, for we are open to receive what you have to say. God, we thank you for dressing us in your full armor and equipping us with all we need today.

Ignite the fire inside of us to do something with what you gave us to work with. Thank you for results coming from the efforts we put forth. Shift our minds to agree with your word according to Luke 11:9-10: *"And I say unto you, Ask, and it shall be given you; seek, and ye shall find; knock, and it shall be opened unto you. For every one that asketh receiveth; and he that seeketh findeth; and to him that knocketh it shall be opened."*

Remove the barriers that block our belief so that what we ask in Jesus's name will be done. Make this day productive, bearing much good fruit. We decree and declare that what we speak shall manifest. In Jesus's name we pray. Amen.

Stimulating Thought

Thank God in advance for the things you are expecting. You don't have to wait until after it manifests to praise him. He appreciates and dwells in the midst of your praise. He identifies with your praise and the unique way you present it to him. It should not be the way anyone else offers it, just as when children have different ways they show love and appreciation to their parents. Show God the love you have for him in your own unique way.

Reflections

Day 46

Great morning, God. Great morning, Jesus. Great morning, Holy Spirit. Thank you, God, for this day that you have made, and we are glad and rejoicing in it. Forgive us, God, for the things we have said, done, thought, and felt that are not pleasing to you nor lining up with your word.

We come this morning with hearts of thanksgiving for all that you have done and continue to do on our behalf every second. Thank you for waking us up this morning with a right mind. You watched over us all night and touched us with your finger of love this morning. Your grace and mercy have kept us in every area of our lives. We lack no good thing because you provide all our needs according to your riches and glory. Cancel the assignment of the enemy today, for he desires to sabotage your plan for our lives. Increase our faith and confidence to pursue, overtake, and recover all the things we need to acquire. Since no weapon that forms against us shall prosper, we thank you for sending every demon and imp fleeing in the name of Jesus.

Greatness is ahead for our lives even as the opposition has grown immensely. Strengthen us to withstand the storm until we see the manifestation of what you are doing. Prepare our hearts and minds to be in the right condition to receive what you have for us. Let your word according to Romans 12:1-3 penetrate our hearts: *"I beseech you therefore, brethren, by the mercies of God, that ye present your bodies a living sacrifice, holy, acceptable unto God, which is your reasonable service. And be not conformed to this world: but be ye transformed by the renewing of your mind, that ye may prove what is that good, and acceptable, and perfect, will of God. For I say, through the grace given unto me, to every man that is among you, not to think of himself more highly than he ought to think; but to think soberly, according as God hath dealt to every man the measure of faith."*

Keep us humble in all our ways, for we know that every promotion or increase comes from you. Give us more of your Spirit and a greater reflection of your character in our lives. Perfect our praise to be pure to you as a sweet fragrance when it reaches your nostrils. Release your glory in response to the sacrifice of praise offered to you. It is in the name of Jesus that we pray. Amen.

Stimulating Thought

God is amazing in his infinite wisdom as he speaks to us at the right time and with the right words. The Spirit of God will send the right person with the very words or expression we need at any given time. We don't know what God is up to when we think something may seem ridiculous. Someone's deliverance is inside of us, but we must be sensitive and obedient to the Spirit of God when he speaks. We are told that God has chosen the foolish things of the world to confound the wise. No matter how many books someone has read, or the number of degrees they hold, they are still no wiser than God. God can drop nuggets into even a child or uneducated person, and it will be the very thing to bring about what is needed in the lives of others. Be open and don't limit God by keeping him in a box or staying shut up in one yourself. It's time to come out of the box.

Reflections

_____

_____

_____

_____

_____

_____

_____

Day 47

Great morning, God. Great morning, Jesus. Great morning, Holy Spirit. Thank you, God, for this day that you have made, and we are glad and rejoicing in it. Forgive us, God, for the things we have said, done, thought, and felt that are not pleasing to you nor lining up with your word.

Lord, we are available to you as we yield our hearts, minds, and bodies to you. You have given us many tools to use for your glory and we appreciate each one. Sharpen what you have placed in us so it does not become dull.

We acknowledge the word to let it penetrate our hearts according to Psalm 51:1-15: *"Have mercy upon me, O God, according to thy loving-kindness: according unto the multitude of thy tender mercies blot out my transgressions. Wash me thoroughly from mine iniquity, and cleanse me from my sin. For I acknowledge my transgressions: and my sin is ever before me. Against thee, thee only, have I sinned, and done this evil in thy sight: that thou mightest be justified when thou speakest, and be clear when thou judgest. Behold, I was shapen in iniquity; and in sin did my mother conceive me. Behold, thou desirest truth in the inward parts: and in the hidden part thou shalt make me to know wisdom. Purge me with hyssop, and I shall be clean: wash me, and I shall be whiter than snow. Make me to hear joy and gladness; that the bones which thou hast broken may rejoice. Hide thy face from my sins, and blot out all mine iniquities. Create in me a clean heart, O God; and renew a right spirit within me. Cast me not away from thy presence; and take not thy holy spirit from me. Restore unto me the joy of thy salvation; and uphold me with thy free spirit. Then will I teach transgressors thy ways; and sinners shall be converted unto thee. Deliver me from bloodguiltiness, O God, thou God of my salvation: and my tongue shall sing aloud of thy righteousness. O Lord, open thou my lips; and my mouth shall show forth thy praise."*

Filter out everything that needs to be removed from us so we can be effective in the kingdom. Erase the blemishes that rest upon our lives so that nothing will block or turn others away from Jesus because of what they see in us. Check us, Holy Spirit, and correct any imbalance in our lives. Don't let us be comfortable while knowingly living in sin by performing acts and speaking things that directly go against your principles. Bring our flesh under subjection to your Spirit. It is in the name of Jesus we do pray. Amen.

Stimulating Thought

Do you have moments that you just say "Hmm" to things that children say or even what you yourself have said as a child of God? Most parents are embarrassed when their children tell a lie or they find out their kids have misbehaved outside of their presence. We are all children of the Most High God, and when we lie, that affects God. The world is watching our lives when we profess Christ. That is a tall statement to make and then not back up. Live a life reflective of who Christ really is. He is the joy and strength in our lives. He is the mother and father to the parentless. He is the husband and wife to those without a spouse. He is I AM. Whatever you need him to be, HE IS. Tell the truth and be who you are without hiding behind Christianity, rather than bring shame to the name of Jesus. God appreciates our honesty, and he can work with that far more than if we are not being true to ourselves. He can still use us no matter the state of our lives, but we must have sincere hearts. He knows and still cares for us.

Reflections

Day 48

Great morning, God. Great morning, Jesus. Great morning, Holy Spirit. Thank you, God, for this day that you have made, and we are glad and rejoicing in it. Forgive us, God, for the things we have said, done, thought, and felt that are not pleasing to you nor lining up with your word.

Thank you for providing your word to us for reading and meditating each day. Let us rightly divide the word of truth to penetrate our hearts and minds that we might be transformed beings. Shift us to a new dimension concerning spiritual things to hear and see things the way you are presenting them. Let us catch hold of the revelation you are giving as you sharpen our discernment for the spirits dwelling among us every day.

Position us with the right people today for divine connections to be made, salvation to come, and impartation to take place. Thank you for reminding us of your position according to your word in Isaiah 43:15-22 (NLT): *"I am the Lord, your Holy One, Israel's Creator and King. I am the Lord, who opened a way through the waters, making a dry path through the sea. I called forth the mighty army of Egypt with all its chariots and horses. I drew them beneath the waves, and they drowned, their lives snuffed out like a smoldering candlewick. But forget all that—it is nothing compared to what I am going to do. For I am about to do something new. See, I have already begun! Do you not see it? I will make a pathway through the wilderness. I will create rivers in the dry wasteland. The wild animals in the fields will thank me, the jackals and owls, too, for giving them water in the desert. Yes, I will make rivers in the dry wasteland so my chosen people can be refreshed. I have made Israel for myself, and they will someday honor me before the whole world. But, dear family of Jacob, you refuse to ask for my help. You have grown tired of me, O Israel!"*

Draw us close to you, Lord. You are our source and you provide us with many resources each day of our lives. Keep us mindful of our purpose: to give you glory. It is not about what others do or don't do. It is not even about how others treat us. It is all about the love of Jesus. Increase the love we have for you and others. It is in the name of Jesus we pray. Amen.

Stimulating Thought

We know that there is a purpose for each of our lives. Sometimes we are not yet sure of that purpose, but nonetheless there still is one. Take time to ask God to show you the purpose he has for your life. When you receive the answer, give him a yes. Not a partial yes by half doing it, but a full yes by committing your heart to the assignment. There is more at stake than just your disobedience. Others' lives are at stake if you don't fulfill the purpose for your life. Is there any difference between premeditating the murder of someone and simply allowing them to die because you don't want to obey the assignment God has given you to encourage them? At some point in each of our lives, we've met someone who spoke to us or did a kind act to keep us alive when we wanted to just throw in the towel. Choose to promote life.

Reflections

_____

_____

_____

_____

_____

_____

_____

Day 49

Great morning, God. Great morning, Jesus. Great morning, Holy Spirit. Thank you, God, for this day that you have made, and we are glad and rejoicing in it. Forgive us, God, for the things we have said, done, thought, and felt that are not pleasing to you nor lining up with your word.

We are grateful for this brand-new day you have given us to carry out a little more of the purpose for our lives. Tune our ears today to hear with clarity and not fall prey to the distractions placed before us even as the enemy attempts to get us to abort our assignment. Remove all heaviness and tiredness from us to be free in you today.

Renew our minds to be open and receptive of the truth of your word according to Psalm 85:4-13: *"Turn us, O God of our salvation, and cause thine anger toward us to cease. Wilt thou be angry with us for ever? wilt thou draw out thine anger to all generations? Wilt thou not revive us again: that thy people may rejoice in thee? Shew us thy mercy, O Lord, and grant us thy salvation. I will hear what God the Lord will speak: for he will speak peace unto his people, and to his saints: but let them not turn again to folly. Surely his salvation is nigh them that fear him; that glory may dwell in our land. Mercy and truth are met together; righteousness and peace have kissed each other. Truth shall spring out of the earth; and righteousness shall look down from heaven. Yea, the Lord shall give that which is good; and our land shall yield her increase. Righteousness shall go before him; and shall set us in the way of his steps."*

Gracious Father, we thank you for the plan you already have in place on our behalf. We accept all that you have made available to us and go out with great expectations to impact the kingdom today. Keep us in a grateful posture as we consider how blessed we are. In the mighty name of Jesus we pray this day. Amen.

Stimulating Thought

Facing, accepting, and applying the truth is not always easy. It is the best thing to do but not the easiest. When we continue to carry false burdens and untruths, the weight becomes heavy for us. As we read the word and apply it by putting on the garment of praise, the weight lifts. The challenge has been made for truth to prevail in our lives. God desires for us to operate in the present truth. The great thing about the truth is that it speaks for itself. For every lie told, another has to be told to cover it. There is a way to avoid all that work simply by doing it God's way. Whatever we speak shall manifest. So speak the truth over your life and situations based on the promises of God and they shall come to pass.

Reflections

_____

_____

_____

_____

_____

_____

Day 50

Great morning, God. Great morning, Jesus. Great morning, Holy Spirit. Thank you, God, for this day that you have made, and we are glad and rejoicing in it. Forgive us, God, for the things we have said, done, thought, and felt that are not pleasing to you nor lining up with your word.

Thank you, God, for giving us choices in life. We choose to worship you in spirit and in truth. We choose to love and not hate. We choose to forgive and not hold on to any jealousy. We choose Jesus over all that the world has to offer.

Thank you for your word according to Matthew 16:24-28: *"Then said Jesus unto his disciples, If any man will come after me, let him deny himself, and take up his cross, and follow me. For whosoever will save his life shall lose it: and whosoever will lose his life for my sake shall find it. For what is a man profited, if he shall gain the whole world, and lose his own soul? or what shall a man give in exchange for his soul? For the Son of man shall come in the glory of his Father with his angels; and then he shall reward every man according to his works. Verily I say unto you, There be some standing here, which shall not taste of death, till they see the Son of man coming in his kingdom."*

We desire more of you, Lord, than what the world offers. Our hearts are desperate for you. Refresh, renew, and revive us. Let everything that comes from us be sweet-smelling in your nostrils as we worship you in spirit and in truth. Thank you in advance for what this day holds according to your will and perfect plan. It is in Jesus's name we do pray. Amen.

Stimulating Thought

Our God said he would provide all our needs according to his riches in glory in Christ Jesus. Therefore, the needs of our bodies, minds, and spirits are being met. We have no reason to walk around in defeat with a "Woe is me" attitude. That is what the enemy wants us to do: to give up and simply die. Victory is ours each day that we wake up because the blood of Jesus still has power and is working for us. Death, hell, and the grave were defeated when Jesus died, stayed in the grave three days, and rose again on the third day. The penalty has been paid and the work is complete for redemption, so rejoice.

Reflections

_____

_____

_____

_____

_____

_____

Day 51

Great morning, God. Great morning, Jesus. Great morning, Holy Spirit. Thank you, God, for this day that you have made, and we are glad and rejoicing in it. Forgive us, God, for the things we have said, done, thought, and felt that are not pleasing to you nor lining up with your word.

This is a new day's journey and we are excited about the path you have set us on today. Daily you load us with many benefits and we thank you that they do not run out. Thank you for your unmerited favor that covers us. We have done nothing to deserve it but you still show us favor. Give us a praying spirit that is unending.

Seal off every crack that would allow the entry of any unclean spirits. We cast down every vain imagination before it begins to marinate in our minds. Thank you for your word assuring us according to Luke 10:16-20: *"He that heareth you heareth me; and he that despiseth you despiseth me; and he that despiseth me despiseth him that sent me. And the seventy returned again with joy, saying, Lord, even the devils are subject unto us through thy name. And he said unto them, I behold Satan as lightning fall from heaven. Behold, I give unto you power to tread on serpents and scorpions, and over all the power of the enemy: and nothing shall by any means hurt you. Notwithstanding in this rejoice not, that the spirits are subject unto you; but rather rejoice, because your names are written in heaven."*

Holy Spirit, rise in us today to walk in boldness to declare the word of the Lord. Thank you for the season of rest we will soon enter to build us up for the next season of labor. Speak to our spirits to give us the strategy necessary to be effective and succeed in advancing the kingdom. It is in the name of Jesus that we pray. Amen.

Stimulating Thought

Be true to who you say you are, all the time, to everyone. We represent God in all things that we do to our family, friends, and coworkers. How are we presenting God to others through our actions and speech? We are the salt of the earth and a light to the world. Pour out the salt necessary for life in your times of fellowship with one another. Be that light to brighten the path you travel so that others along the way will come out of darkness and into the marvelous light. There is always work to be done if we will step up to do it. Souls are waiting to be saved when we show up to share Jesus. Step outside of your comfort zone to reach the lost and show the compassion that has been shown to us by God. It is not about what is convenient, but it is about commitment.

Reflections

Day 52

Great morning, God. Great morning, Jesus. Great morning, Holy Spirit. Thank you, God, for this day that you have made, and we are glad and rejoicing in it. Forgive us, God, for the things we have said, done, thought, and felt that are not pleasing to you nor lining up with your word.

Lord, we love and magnify you. We honor you, God, for reigning over all the earth. Nothing in the earth is hidden from you, for you know all things that take place. Cleanse our hearts and minds of anything impure.

Guide us through this day, Holy Spirit, for the things we should say and do and the places we must go. Keep us humbled and not entangled by the yoke of bondage in this world according to Romans 12:1-3: *"I beseech you therefore, brethren, by the mercies of God, that ye present your bodies a living sacrifice, holy, acceptable unto God, which is your reasonable service. And be not conformed to this world: but be ye transformed by the renewing of your mind, that ye may prove what is that good, and acceptable, and perfect, will of God. For I say, through the grace given unto me, to every man that is among you, not to think of himself more highly than he ought to think; but to think soberly, according as God hath dealt to every man the measure of faith."*

Our spirits leap with anticipation and expectation for what is about to happen today. Speak, Lord, with clarity so that we hear you without any doubt that you are speaking. Move in the hearts of people all around the world with addictions of any sort to be open to you and freed from things of the past tormenting their minds and spirits as they keep dwelling on those things behind them. Uproot from the very core the source of the problem so the addictions will no longer have any power over or effect on their lives. It is in the name of Jesus we do pray. Amen.

Stimulating Thought

We live in a time that requires us to constantly make decisions that affect the rest of our lives. Don't be so quick to make a decision or give an answer that may not be what is necessary to endure for a lifetime. We are told to be swift to hear, slow to speak, slow to wrath. When we are in certain situations, an answer will come as a result of the action taken against us. Even when we are placed in a position to be blessed, we must make sure that the terms are laid out by the Lord. It is okay to sleep on it to hear from God before giving an answer on some things. God does not place us in a position of struggle when he blesses us. The blessings of the Lord make us rich and he adds no sorrow to them. If you go into something having a hard time with it, ask God if it is for you yet. What he has for you is for you. Just know the timing of God.

Reflections

_____

_____

_____

_____

_____

_____

_____

_____

_____

Day 53

Great morning, God. Great morning, Jesus. Great morning, Holy Spirit. Thank you, God, for this day that you have made, and we are glad and rejoicing in it. Forgive us, God, for the things we have said, done, thought, and felt that are not pleasing to you nor lining up with your word.

We come before you humbly asking that you cleanse our hands and purify our hearts. God, you are concerned about every soul, so we come standing in the gap for the lost souls all around the world. Thank you for the mercy that you show us even when we have not done anything to deserve it.

Give us a new level of boldness to step out in faith without hesitation to do the things you have spoken. Thank you for what you will show us as we move in obedience. Your word guides us as it says according to Proverbs 16:1-9: *"The preparations of the heart in man, and the answer of the tongue, is from the Lord. All the ways of a man are clean in his own eyes; but the Lord weigheth the spirits. Commit thy works unto the Lord, and thy thoughts shall be established. The Lord hath made all things for himself: yea, even the wicked for the day of evil. Every one that is proud in heart is an abomination to the Lord: though hand join in hand, he shall not be unpunished. By*

143

mercy and truth iniquity is purged: and by the fear of the Lord men depart from evil. When a man's ways please the Lord, he maketh even his enemies to be at peace with him. Better is a little with righteousness than great revenues without right. A man's heart deviseth his way: but the Lord directeth his steps."

Encourage our souls today to continue on the path you have set us on no matter how hard the way may seem as we travel. God, we recognize that you did not bring us this far to leave us stranded and that there is something great ahead if we continue to press on to arrive. Keep us focused on what is important and keep us from being anxious about the little things. We yield totally to your Holy Spirit today. It is in the name of Jesus that we pray. Amen.

Stimulating Thought

We simply cannot do some things in the natural on our own, and they require God stepping in to do them. Is there anything too hard for God to do? Of course not. Can he do all things? Yes, he can. It is okay to take your hands off of matters and leave them for God to fix. We cannot change people, but God can touch their hearts and allow a different outcome. God can change up the details of situations and make the outcomes totally different from what would have resulted if we would've done what we had in mind. Don't lean to your own understanding and knowledge in matters, but trust God to direct you. Watch the difference in the matter when God steps in.

Reflections

_____

_____

_____

_____

_____

_____

_____

_____

_____

Day 54

Great morning, God. Great morning, Jesus. Great morning, Holy Spirit. Thank you, God, for this day that you have made, and we are glad and rejoicing in it. Forgive us, God, for the things we have said, done, thought, and felt that are not pleasing to you nor lining up with your word.

Thank you for your word fortifying us at all times to rise in the strength needed for every challenge we face. Prepare us mentally for the tactics of the enemy as he engages us in war. We recognize that we are not in a physical battle but rather one of the spirit that must be conquered by the spiritual weapons acquired from the arsenal of your word.

Your word inspires and ignites us as it says according to 2 Timothy 1:6-14: *"Wherefore I put thee in remembrance that thou stir up the gift of God, which is in thee by the putting on of my hands. For God hath not given us the spirit of fear; but of power, and of love, and of a sound mind. Be not thou therefore ashamed of the testimony of our Lord, nor of me his prisoner: but be thou partaker of the afflictions of the gospel according to the power of God; who hath saved us, and called us with an holy calling, not according to our works, but according to his own purpose and grace, which was given us in Christ Jesus before the world began, but is now made manifest by the appearing of our Saviour Jesus Christ, who hath abolished death, and hath brought life and immortality to light through the gospel: whereunto I am appointed a preacher, and an apostle, and a teacher of the Gentiles. For the which cause I also suffer these things: nevertheless I am not ashamed: for I know whom I have believed, and am persuaded that he is able to keep that which I have committed unto him against that day. Hold fast the form of sound words, which thou hast heard of me, in faith and love which is in Christ Jesus. That good thing which was committed unto thee keep by the Holy Ghost which dwelleth in us."*

We are equipped with everything we need to stand and do spiritual battle. We decree and declare that we shall walk in the full authority you have given us and that a manifestation of your power will be demonstrated in every situation we must address today. Every giant will crumple and fall today at the name of Jesus and the command of the word of God. No weapon formed against us will prosper and no sickness shall invade our bodies to overtake us. We are the healed of the Lord walking in divine health. We call forth the healing in our spirits to manifest in our bodies. The walls are coming down and the masks are being removed now in the name of Jesus. It is time for the flesh to sit down to allow the Spirit of God to rise and take the lead. It is so in Jesus's name. Amen.

Stimulating Thought

What do you want God to do on your behalf this day? God said to ask and it shall be given. Do not be afraid to ask God for what is already in your heart. He wants to heal, deliver, and free us. There are no limits or boundaries today. Take the limits off your mind for what you will be bold enough to ask and trust God to do. Simply speak what you desire from God and expect him to move. You will be amazed at the outcome if you will only believe. God is shifting the faith and confidence of his people.

Reflections

_____

_____

_____

_____

_____

_____

_____

Day 55

Great morning, God. Great morning, Jesus. Great morning, Holy Spirit. Thank you, God, for this day that you have made, and we are glad and rejoicing in it. Forgive us, God, for the things we have said, done, thought, and felt that are not pleasing to you nor lining up with your word.

This morning we come with hearts of worship before you. Fill us today as we come before you empty so that you can pour into us. Let the greater works be done in and through us just as you said we would do.

Ignite the power in us to become alive and active as you said according to Ephesians 2:1-10: *"And you hath he quickened, who were dead in trespasses and sins; wherein in time past ye walked according to the course of this world, according to the prince of the power of the air, the spirit that now worketh in the children of disobedience: among whom also we all had our conversation in times past in the lusts of our flesh, fulfilling the desires of the flesh and of the mind; and were by nature the children of wrath, even as others. But God, who is rich in mercy, for his great love wherewith he loved us, even when we were dead in sins, hath quickened us together with Christ, (by grace ye are saved;) and hath raised us up together, and made us sit together in heavenly places in Christ Jesus: that in the ages to come he might shew the exceeding riches of his grace in his kindness toward us through Christ Jesus. For by grace are ye saved through faith; and that not of yourselves: it is the gift of God: not of works, lest any man should boast. For we are his workmanship, created in Christ Jesus unto good works, which God hath before ordained that we should walk in them."*

Thank you for giving us strength and wisdom to walk upright before you as you order our steps. Touch our hearts to walk in obedience and not be slaves to fear. Let boldness rise in us to face the giants in our lives head-on, not allowing them to increase. It is in the name of Jesus that we pray. Amen.

Stimulating Thought

It is time to face certain truths in life, beginning with taking a look in the mirror. Sometimes it is easy to see shortcomings and mistakes when it comes to other people, but can we accept where we have imperfections within and be willing to get fixed? The greatest tool to fix us is the word of God, filling us to do a makeover from the inside out. We function and live much better when we are fixed.

Reflections

_____

_____

_____

_____

_____

_____

_____

_____

Day 56

Great morning, God. Great morning, Jesus. Great morning, Holy Spirit. Thank you, God, for this day that you have made, and we are glad and rejoicing in it. Forgive us, God, for the things we have said, done, thought, and felt that are not pleasing to you nor lining up with your word.

We come with our hands lifted to you, humbled in a posture of worship. Our eyes are lifted up to you as the only help that we know. Thank you for direction as you guide us in the paths of righteousness.

Renew our minds and give us a paradigm shift. Remove the things from our thoughts that should not reside in our minds as we cast down every vain imagination. Proverbs 23:3-12 guides our thinking as it says: *"Be not desirous of his dainties: for they are deceitful meat. Labour not to be rich: cease from thine own wisdom. Wilt thou set thine eyes upon that which is not? for riches certainly make themselves wings; they fly away as an eagle toward heaven. Eat thou not the bread of him that hath an evil eye, neither desire thou his dainty meats: for as he thinketh in his heart, so is he: Eat and drink, saith he to thee; but his heart is not with thee. The morsel which thou hast eaten shalt thou vomit up, and lose thy sweet words. Speak not in the ears of a fool: for he will despise the wisdom of thy words. Remove not the old landmark; and enter not into the fields of the fatherless: for their redeemer is mighty; he shall plead their cause with thee. Apply thine heart unto instruction, and thine ears to the words of knowledge."*

Strengthen us in the areas of weakness. Connect us with individuals who are stronger than us in various areas so as to impart helpful nuggets for us to live by in moments of weakness. Open our ears and hearts to receive what you are speaking in this hour. Cover the earth, Lord, for the light to outshine every dark place. It is in the name of Jesus that we pray. Amen.

Stimulating Thought

What do you do when you don't know what to do or what direction to take? It is so easy to just give up, but what have you accomplished? Seek the face of God and he will answer and direct you. Be willing to accept his instructions and follow them. God can see further than we can. He will also give us eagle-eye vision as we become tuned to his voice to guide us.

Reflections

_____

_____

_____

_____

_____

_____

_____

Day 57

Great morning, God. Great morning, Jesus. Great morning, Holy Spirit. Thank you, God, for this day that you have made, and we are glad and rejoicing in it. Forgive us, God, for the things we have said, done, thought, and felt that are not pleasing to you nor lining up with your word.

This morning we come before you with pure hearts, humbled in your presence. You already see and know all things concerning us, so we are transparent before you today. Lift every weight that is upon us. Destroy every chain restraining us.

Free our minds from all confusion and chaos. We cast down every vain imagination. Thank you for your word according to 2 Corinthians 10:2-16: *"But I beseech you, that I may not be bold when I am present with that confidence, wherewith I think to be bold against some, which think of us as if we walked according to the flesh. For though we walk in the flesh, we do not war after the flesh: (For the weapons of our warfare are not carnal, but mighty through God to the pulling down of strong holds;) casting down imaginations, and every high thing that exalteth itself against the knowledge of God, and bringing into captivity every thought to the obedience of Christ;*

and having in a readiness to revenge all disobedience, when your obe-
dience is fulfilled. Do ye look on things after the outward appearance?
if any man trust to himself that he is Christ's, let him of himself think
this again, that, as he is Christ's, even so are we Christ's. For though
I should boast somewhat more of our authority, which the Lord hath
given us for edification, and not for your destruction, I should not be
ashamed: that I may not seem as if I would terrify you by letters. For
his letters, say they, are weighty and powerful; but his bodily presence
is weak, and his speech contemptible. Let such an one think this, that,
such as we are in word by letters when we are absent, such will we be
also in deed when we are present. For we dare not make ourselves of
the number, or compare ourselves with some that commend themselves:
but they measuring themselves by themselves, and comparing them-
selves among themselves, are not wise. But we will not boast of things
without our measure, but according to the measure of the rule which
God hath distributed to us, a measure to reach even unto you. For we
stretch not ourselves beyond our measure, as though we reached not
unto you: for we are come as far as to you also in preaching the gospel
of Christ: not boasting of things without our measure, that is, of other
men's labours; but having hope, when your faith is increased, that we
shall be enlarged by you according to our rule abundantly, to preach
the gospel in the regions beyond you, and not to boast in another man's
line of things made ready to our hand."

Increase our ammunition as we spend time in your word, praying and worshipping you. Break up the fallow ground that remains
uncultivated and prepare it for reseeding with your word. Mend
broken hearts severed because of discord in family relations and situations today. Restore, refresh, revive, and regenerate everything back
to the state for which it was created to function. Remove feelings of
resentment for any past hurts and fill hearts with love. Thank you
for being ever present in all things and for being available to call on
anytime. It is in the name of Jesus we pray. Amen.

Stimulating Thought

Whose weight are you carrying in addition to your own? Sometimes we find our lives being out of balance due to having too many things on our plate that do not belong to us. God is very specific in his directives for our lives. He said to be careful for nothing but in all things to go to him in prayer. That simply means don't carry excessive baggage that is not yours. He did not equip or design us to carry extra things. We were created for his glory and for fellowship with him. Cast every one of your cares upon him, including your spouse, your children, the rest of your family, your job, how you will live from day to day, and all that is going on in this world. God wants to refocus your life and give you balance. Let him do it. Just exhale, and with every release of breath, let go of another extra weight you are carrying.

Reflections

_____

_____

_____

_____

_____

_____

Day 58

Great morning, God. Great morning, Jesus. Great morning, Holy Spirit. Thank you, God, for this day that you have made, and we are glad and rejoicing in it. Forgive us, God, for the things we have said, done, thought, and felt that are not pleasing to you nor lining up with your word.

We come this morning rejoicing in you for being our God. You are the God who rules and reigns over all the earth—the God of Abraham, Isaac, and Jacob. The battles we face daily are not ours, but they belong to you, God, because you fight on our behalf.

Praise comes from us continually because we already know you have every situation worked out on our behalf. There is praise in our spirit before the victory even comes. Thank you in advance for the walls that are coming down because we speak to them in the name of Jesus. Shift the atmosphere for breakthrough to come, for you have encamped angels around us for the blessings to come through every barrier set by the enemy. Lord, you know the situations before they even arise in our lives, so we thank you for the strength you have placed in us to face them. Thank you for your word according to Isaiah 26:1-4 (NLT): *"In that day, everyone in the land of Judah will sing this song: Our city is strong! We are surrounded by the walls of God's salvation.*

Open the gates to all who are righteous; allow the faithful to enter. You will keep in perfect peace all who trust in you, all whose thoughts are fixed on you! Trust in the Lord always, for the Lord God is the eternal Rock."

Lord, you are good and your mercy endures forever. We thank you for the covering of your grace and not being bound by the law. Holy Spirit, have your way in us as boldness rises in us today. It is in the name of Jesus that we do pray. Amen.

Stimulating Thought

Are you flexible to bend at any given moment? Sometimes situations arise in life that we are not prepared for, nor do we desire them. And new situations certainly don't always wait to arise until the current ones are over. We must be willing to shift position for whatever situation we find ourselves in and allow God to perform miracles while we are there. Some situations come simply to make and develop us for where we are headed. Be open to what God is doing in you to prepare you for the greater thing ahead. Your latter things shall be greater than the former. Rejoice in the good and bad times because God is still in position upon the throne. He knows our DNA and will put no more on each individual than they can bear.

Reflections

_____

_____

_____

_____

_____

_____

_____

Day 59

Great morning, God. Great morning, Jesus. Great morning, Holy Spirit. Thank you, God, for this day that you have made, and we are glad and rejoicing in it. Forgive us, God, for the things we have said, done, thought, and felt that are not pleasing to you nor lining up with your word.

This morning we come before you with a sacrifice of praise. We seek you early this morning while you may be found. Keep our hearts and minds set on you so that we may be in perfect peace. We decree and declare that we shall live and not die because we are redeemed by the blood of Jesus. You gave us the ability to speak those things to manifest, so help us to speak only what is good according to your word. Let us not dwell on bad or negative things, because all things are possible through Christ who strengthens us.

Confidently we stand, knowing who we are in you. We are the head, not the tail. We are the first and not the last. We are the righteousness of God because Christ took on all our sin. We are the just and we live by faith as more than conquerors through Jesus. Reveal to us any areas in which we have denied Christ or left him out of our lives unintentionally so that we will no longer do that. Your word gives an account of the actions leading to the arrest of Jesus, as it says according to Matthew 26:31-39: *"Then saith Jesus unto them, All ye shall be offended because of me this night: for it is written, I will smite the shepherd, and the sheep of the flock shall be scattered abroad. But after I am risen again, I will go before you into Galilee. Peter answered and said unto him, Though all men shall be offended because of thee, yet will I never be offended. Jesus said unto him, Verily I say unto thee, That this night, before the cock crow, thou shalt deny me thrice. Peter said unto him, Though I should die with thee, yet will I not deny thee. Likewise also said all the disciples. Then cometh Jesus with them unto a place called Gethsemane, and saith unto the disciples, Sit ye here, while I go and pray yonder. And he took with him Peter and the two sons of Zebedee, and began to be sorrowful and very heavy. Then saith he unto them, My soul is exceeding sorrowful, even unto death: tarry ye here, and watch with me. And he went a little further, and fell on his face, and prayed, saying, O my Father, if it be possible, let this cup pass from me: nevertheless not as I will, but as thou wilt."*

We thank you for the emotions you have allowed us to see in Jesus as a reminder of his humanity. Today we face our own emotional truths. Thank you for your Holy Spirit giving us strength and discernment to know when to release our feelings and when to hold back. It is in the name of Jesus that we do pray. Amen.

Stimulating Thought

As the old saying goes, "You can't judge a book by its cover." Rather, you must open it up and read it to know and understand the content. The same applies when it comes to knowing God and other people. We cannot know or develop a relationship with God without spending time with him and getting to know who he is. Reading the word, praying, and worshipping are ways to spend time with God and develop that relationship. As we build our relationship with God, he gives us greater discernment for the spirits that dwell in others around us or when we meet new people. We are not here to judge one another, for God is the only judge. We are here to edify and build up one another.

Reflections

_____

_____

_____

_____

_____

_____

_____

Day 60

Great morning, God. Great morning, Jesus. Great morning, Holy Spirit. Thank you, God, for this day that you have made, and we are glad and rejoicing in it. Forgive us, God, for the things we have said, done, thought, and felt that are not pleasing to you nor lining up with your word.

We come with lifted hands to give you glory and praise. It is another day that you have kept us, Lord, and we are glad for the journey. God, you are amazing with the miracles you perform every day as you keep us alive and breathing. Thank you for peace and uncommon favor resting upon us today.

As we think on Jesus and reflect on all that he faced during the days leading up to his crucifixion, our souls cry "Hallelujah!" for what he has done for each of us. As Matthew 26:40-56 illustrates: *"And he cometh unto the disciples, and findeth them asleep, and saith unto Peter, What, could ye not watch with me one hour? Watch and pray, that ye enter not into temptation: the spirit indeed is willing, but the flesh is weak. He went away again the second time, and prayed, saying, O my Father, if this cup may not pass away from me, except I drink it, thy will be done. And he came and found them asleep again: for their eyes were heavy. And he left them, and went away again, and prayed the third time, saying the same words. Then cometh he to his disciples, and saith unto them, Sleep on now, and take your rest: behold, the hour is at hand, and the Son of man is betrayed into the hands of sinners. Rise, let us be going: behold, he is at hand that doth betray me. And while he yet spake, lo, Judas, one of the twelve, came, and with him a great multitude with swords and staves, from the chief priests and elders of the people. Now he that betrayed him gave them a sign, saying, Whomsoever I shall kiss, that same is he: hold him fast. And forthwith he came to Jesus, and said, Hail, master; and kissed him. And Jesus said unto him, Friend, wherefore art thou come? Then came they, and laid hands on Jesus, and took him. And, behold, one of them which were with Jesus stretched out his hand, and drew his sword, and struck a servant of the high priest's, and smote off his ear. Then said Jesus unto him, Put up again thy sword into his place: for all they that take the sword shall perish with the sword. Thinkest thou that I cannot now pray to my Father, and he shall presently give me more than twelve legions of angels? But how then shall the scriptures be fulfilled, that thus it must be? In that same hour said Jesus to the multitudes, Are ye come out as against a thief with swords and staves for to take me? I sat daily with you teaching in the temple, and ye laid no hold on me. But all this was done, that the scriptures of the prophets might be fulfilled. Then all the disciples forsook him, and fled."*

Keep us revived and focused on the things that pertain to you, God. Let us not reduce our commitment to you and walk away. You are always with us no matter what we face. No decision is made in the earth without you being aware of it, God, and we thank you for what you allow and how far you will let a thing go before you step in. Just as the scripture was being fulfilled when they came to arrest Jesus, the script that has been written for our lives is playing out each day we live and experience all that we go through. Thank you for the beautiful outcome of what appeared to be trouble and chaos in the life of Jesus. It was all for your glory to restore the relationship between you and man. It is in the name of Jesus that we do pray. Amen.

Stimulating Thought

We have likely all heard the cliché, "The mind is a terrible thing to waste." If that be the case, why do we continue to do it? We lend our minds to the thoughts that Satan authors when we entertain negative conversations, watch inappropriate things on-screen, and read the contents of written pieces that suck the life from us rather than inspire us. A young preacher once shared a message titled "Get Your Mind Right," and she touched on points to bring our minds into alignment with the mind of Christ. You might wonder, "Well, how do I do that?" First, we must be a willing vessel to yield to God. His word is available to us in so many formats that no one can use the excuse of not being able to hear or read the word. Meditate on it day and night to penetrate your spirit, body, and mind. The more that you take in, the greater change you'll experience in submitting your thoughts to God.

Reflections

_____

_____

_____

_____

_____

_____

_____

Day 61

Great morning, God. Great morning, Jesus. Great morning, Holy Spirit. Thank you, God, for this day that you have made, and we are glad and rejoicing in it. Forgive us, God, for the things we have said, done, thought, and felt that are not pleasing to you nor lining up with your word.

Lord, we come to worship and adore you today. We exalt you, Lord, and bless your name. Our words cannot do enough to express our gratitude for you. Our hearts are humbled as we come in a posture of repentance. We bow down to worship you, for your name is above every other name.

Thank you for your obedience through the entire process you had to go through to save us. We honor you for enduring until the end according to the scripture in Luke 23:34-48: *"Then said Jesus, Father, forgive them; for they know not what they do. And they parted his raiment, and cast lots. And the people stood beholding. And the rulers also with them derided him, saying, He saved others; let him save himself, if he be Christ, the chosen of God. And the soldiers also mocked him, coming to him, and offering him vinegar, and saying, If thou be the king of the Jews, save thyself. And a superscription also was written over him in letters of Greek, and Latin, and Hebrew, This Is The King*

Of The Jews. And one of the malefactors which were hanged railed on him, saying, If thou be Christ, save thyself and us. But the other answering rebuked him, saying, Dost not thou fear God, seeing thou art in the same condemnation? And we indeed justly; for we receive the due reward of our deeds: but this man hath done nothing amiss. And he said unto Jesus, Lord, remember me when thou comest into thy kingdom. And Jesus said unto him, Verily I say unto thee, Today shalt thou be with me in paradise. And it was about the sixth hour, and there was a darkness over all the earth until the ninth hour. And the sun was darkened, and the veil of the temple was rent in the midst. And when Jesus had cried with a loud voice, he said, Father, into thy hands I commend my spirit: and having said thus, he gave up the ghost. Now when the centurion saw what was done, he glorified God, saying, Certainly this was a righteous man. And all the people that came together to that sight, beholding the things which were done, smote their breasts, and returned."

Forgive us for the daily rejection that takes place when we do things that are contrary to your will or that bring shame to your name. You still love us in spite of this and we thank you. The ransom you paid is priceless and no amount can ever be placed on what you gave to set us free. Let this be a day like no other as we reflect on all that you have done and what you will do this day as hearts around the world are penetrated. It is in the name of Jesus that we do pray. Amen.

Stimulating Thought

Are you saved or just safe? Consider for a moment the day that Jesus died upon the cross. There was nothing good about the treatment he received, but sacrificing himself so that we might live is the good that comes from this. The question of "saved or safe" helps us to see where our hearts are. He died so that we would have the choice to be free to live a holy life before God. We are all safe no matter what because he died and his blood covers us all. We are saved because he rose again, and we can confess and invite him to be our Lord and

Savior. Sometimes we know we're under grace and take the easy route to be on the safe side, hiding behind God's Word to continue in our sin, confessing that all have sinned and fall short of the glory as it says in Romans 3:23. Yes, that is a true statement, but we have a choice to stay in a fallen state or get up and walk out our salvation. It is not a debate or a challenge. We simply must choose to live for Christ or to continue in a life of sin. It is a process, but it begins with having a made-up mind and a purpose and desire in our hearts to live right.

Reflections

_____

_____

_____

_____

_____

_____

_____

Day 62

Great morning, God. Great morning, Jesus. Great morning, Holy Spirit. Thank you, God, for this day that you have made, and we are glad and rejoicing in it. Forgive us, God, for the things we have said, done, thought, and felt that are not pleasing to you nor lining up with your word.

All power belongs to you, God, and we thank you for doing the impossible in our lives as we come to you in faith. You see all who are sick and you said by the stripes of Jesus we are healed. We decree and declare that foreign substances in the bloodstream, muscles, bones, joints, and organs will dissolve and that our bodies will rise healed in the name of Jesus.

Destroy shackles in the minds of people who have entertained the voice of Satan, and let them cast down every vain imagination. Lord, deliver us like only you can from the strongholds and generational curses that hold individuals captive. Your word establishes the strength of its power as it says in 1 John 5:4-15: *"For whatsoever is born of God overcometh the world: and this is the victory that overcometh the world, even our faith. Who is he that overcometh the world, but he that believeth that Jesus is the Son of God? This is he that came by water and blood, even Jesus Christ; not by water only, but by water and blood. And it is the Spirit that beareth witness, because the Spirit is truth. For there are three that bear record in heaven, the Father, the Word, and the Holy Ghost: and these three are one. And there are three that bear witness in earth, the Spirit, and the water, and the blood: and these three agree in one. If we receive the witness of men, the witness of God is greater: for this is the witness of God which he hath testified of his Son. He that believeth on the Son of God hath the witness in himself: he that believeth not God hath made him a liar; because he believeth not the record that God gave of his Son. And this is the record, that God hath given to us eternal life, and this life is in his Son. He that hath the Son hath life; and he that hath not the Son of God hath not life. These things have I written unto you that believe on the name of the Son of God; that ye may know that ye have eternal life, and that ye may believe on the name of the Son of God. And this is the confidence that we have in him, that, if we ask any thing according to his will, he heareth us: And if we know that he hear us, whatsoever we ask, we know that we have the petitions that we desired of him."*

We will open our mouths to release declarations and decrees that shall manifest in our lives and the lives of others. Increase is coming in our spirits, health, and finances. Clarity is coming in our hearing and vision. It is so in the name of Jesus. Amen.

Stimulating Thought

Are you confident in the word of God and the name of Jesus? Day and night speak over yourself what the word says concerning you until you see those things manifest. Declare the promises of God, because he honors his word. Speak life for others when they are weak and wavering in their faith. God has given us a measure of grace to do certain things. Are you coming up to that measure or are you falling short? Meditate on that today and come up to the place you are supposed to be.

Reflections

_____

_____

_____

_____

_____

_____

_____

Day 63

Great morning, God. Great morning, Jesus. Great morning, Holy Spirit. Thank you, God, for this day that you have made, and we are glad and rejoicing in it. Forgive us, God, for the things we have said, done, thought, and felt that are not pleasing to you nor lining up with your word.

Thank you for a new day to worship and praise you for being our God. Renew our thinking to line up with your word and to dwell on good things. Let fresh oil flow in our lives for a new anointing to come upon us.

This day we decree and declare that miracles shall manifest in the physical body as the spirit yields to your will to receive what you have in store for us. Doors shall open that no man can shut. Breakthrough is arriving, which even the devil can't block. Your word establishes according to Galatians 3:5-18: *"He therefore that ministereth to you the Spirit, and worketh miracles among you, doeth he it by the works of the law, or by the hearing of faith? Even as Abraham believed God, and it was accounted to him for righteousness. Know ye therefore that they which are of faith, the same are the children of Abraham. And the scripture, foreseeing that God would justify the heathen through faith, preached before the gospel unto Abraham, saying, In thee shall*

all nations be blessed. So then they which be of faith are blessed with faithful Abraham. For as many as are of the works of the law are under the curse: for it is written, Cursed is every one that continueth not in all things which are written in the book of the law to do them. But that no man is justified by the law in the sight of God, it is evident: for, The just shall live by faith. And the law is not of faith: but, The man that doeth them shall live in them. Christ hath redeemed us from the curse of the law, being made a curse for us: for it is written, Cursed is every one that hangeth on a tree: that the blessing of Abraham might come on the Gentiles through Jesus Christ; that we might receive the promise of the Spirit through faith. Brethren, I speak after the manner of men; Though it be but a man's covenant, yet if it be confirmed, no man disannulleth, or addeth thereto. Now to Abraham and his seed were the promises made. He saith not, And to seeds, as of many; but as of one, And to thy seed, which is Christ. And this I say, that the covenant, that was confirmed before of God in Christ, the law, which was four hundred and thirty years after, cannot disannul, that it should make the promise of none effect. For if the inheritance be of the law, it is no more of promise: but God gave it to Abraham by promise."

We believe all your promises and accept them for our lives. We expect a turnaround in situations today, for we are victorious and not defeated. Increase our faith as we are moved from fear to action, for you have shifted the atmosphere to make room for our moves. It is so, and in the name of Jesus we pray. Amen.

Stimulating Thought

Do feel like others watch you to see how you will respond to life situations so they can gauge their own actions based on what you do? Know that you are chosen for a time such as this to make a difference in the lives of others by your witness. Sometimes it is just the little things you say or do that will impact the lives of those around you. People you don't even realize are watching may be taking the most interest in your life. For some, you may be the only example of Christ they will see to draw them to salvation. Let God use you freely as the Holy Spirit moves and speaks through you. As God is moving for those around you to see him in you, a work is being done to improve your life as well.

Reflections

_____

_____

_____

_____

_____

_____

_____

Day 64

Great morning, God. Great morning, Jesus. Great morning, Holy Spirit. Thank you, God, for this day that you have made, and we are glad and rejoicing in it. Forgive us, God, for the things we have said, done, thought, and felt that are not pleasing to you nor lining up with your word.

Lord, we worship and adore your name today. We lift your name on high and praise you. God, we honor you for being our Lord and Savior. Thank you for all things in our lives happening at your appointed time.

We surrender all to you, Lord, as we think about all that you have done and continue to do for us daily. Let the word according to 1 Peter 4:1-13 sink deep into our spirits: *"Forasmuch then as Christ hath suffered for us in the flesh, arm yourselves likewise with the same mind: for he that hath suffered in the flesh hath ceased from sin; that he no longer should live the rest of his time in the flesh to the lusts of men, but to the will of God. For the time past of our life may suffice us to have wrought the will of the Gentiles, when we walked in lasciviousness, lusts, excess of wine, revellings, banquetings, and abominable idolatries: wherein they think it strange that ye run not with them to the same excess of riot, speaking evil of you: who shall give account to him that is ready to judge the quick and the dead. For this cause was the gospel preached also to them that are dead, that they might be judged according to men in the flesh, but live according to God in the spirit. But the end of all things is at hand: be ye therefore sober, and watch unto prayer. And above all things have fervent charity among yourselves: for charity shall cover the multitude of sins. Use hospitality one to another without grudging. As every man hath received the gift, even so minister the same one to another, as good stewards of the manifold grace of God. If any man speak, let him speak as the oracles of God; if any man minister, let him do it as of the ability which God giveth: that God in all things may be glorified through Jesus Christ, to whom be praise and dominion for ever and ever. Amen. Beloved, think it not strange concerning the fiery trial which is to try you, as though some strange thing happened unto you: but rejoice, inasmuch as ye are partakers of Christ's sufferings; that, when his glory shall be revealed, ye may be glad also with exceeding joy."*

We yield to the transforming power of your word and Holy Spirit. Thank you for the noticeable changes taking place in our lives as we turn away from past things and advance toward the new things you have for us. It is in the name of Jesus we pray. Amen.

Stimulating Thought

Have you ever felt stuck in time right in the middle of an awkward moment and nothing seemed to be moving? Do not be dismayed. God is still watching over all that is taking place. During our growth we face some uncomfortable moments. In the natural, growth spurts sometimes hurt or feel odd. Spiritually we face discomfort as we grow and adjust to how God is shaping who we will become. Do not be afraid to become who God said you really are.

Reflections

_____

_____

_____

_____

_____

_____

_____

Day 65

Great morning, God. Great morning, Jesus. Great morning, Holy Spirit. Thank you, God, for this day that you have made, and we are glad and rejoicing in it. Forgive us, God, for the things we have said, done, thought, and felt that are not pleasing to you nor lining up with your word.

Lord, we come with thankful and humble hearts today. We bow down to worship you, heavenly Father. Every vain imagination is cast down and destroyed in our minds. The chains are falling off every area of our lives where we have been bound. Scales are coming off blinded spiritual eyes, and impaired hearing is being restored and sharpened.

Give us revelation knowledge as the word becomes alive to us and active in us. Speak to us according to your word in Ephesians 3:2-12: *"If ye have heard of the dispensation of the grace of God which is given me to you-ward: how that by revelation he made known unto me the mystery; (as I wrote afore in few words, whereby, when ye read, ye may understand my knowledge in the mystery of Christ) which in other ages was not made known unto the sons of men, as it is now revealed unto his holy apostles and prophets by the Spirit; that the Gentiles should be fellowheirs, and of the same body, and partakers of his promise in Christ by the gospel:*

whereof I was made a minister, according to the gift of the grace of God given unto me by the effectual working of his power. Unto me, who am less than the least of all saints, is this grace given, that I should preach among the Gentiles the unsearchable riches of Christ; and to make all men see what is the fellowship of the mystery, which from the beginning of the world hath been hid in God, who created all things by Jesus Christ: to the intent that now unto the principalities and powers in heavenly places might be known by the church the manifold wisdom of God, according to the eternal purpose which he purposed in Christ Jesus our Lord: in whom we have boldness and access with confidence by the faith of him."

Prepare and condition our hearts to receive sound doctrine and reject anything unsound that does not line up with your word. Open our hearts to receive love as well as to give it to everyone we encounter, to cover the multitude of situations that try to arise. Thank you for this being a wonderful day we will spend with you, Father God. Our spirits leap with anticipation and expectation for something great taking place in the atmosphere today. It is in the name of Jesus we pray. Amen.

Stimulating Thought

When trouble and storms rise in life, our emotions sometimes get the better of us. There is no situation or storm that God is not already aware of before it happens. Nothing just happens without his permission being given. In the book of Job, Satan went before the Lord twice seeking whom he could test in the earth. The Lord suggested Job because he already knew Job's heart and what he was made of. God already knows our hearts and what we are made of because he put everything in us. Job's response to the trouble was not to curse God and die, to fall out having a fit, or to slip into a state of depression. Job worshipped God in his trial. When God allows you to face difficult situations, worship him for getting you through that moment. It is okay to have strong feelings about our situations, but don't let them destroy you. God is always with us, even when it seems like all hell is breaking loose and the demons and imps are on our trail. Know that God is in the midst of it. This is the time to use the tools in your spiritual tool kit. Don't let them get rusty for lack of use. Oil those babies and put them to use through worship, prayer, and praise.

Reflections

Day 66

Great morning, God. Great morning, Jesus. Great morning, Holy Spirit. Thank you, God, for this day that you have made, and we are glad and rejoicing in it. Forgive us, God, for the things we have said, done, thought, and felt that are not pleasing to you nor lining up with your word.

God, you are great and deserve all our praise. You are blessing us even now as we start our day. The blood of Jesus covers us over two thousand years after his death, burial, and resurrection. That same blood sets us free and keeps us in a posture of victory over all the things Satan uses to come against us. None of the enemy's weapons formed against us shall prosper.

We decree today that our bodies shall line up with the word of God and function the way they were created to. Thank you, God, for our brains having the proper fluid to think and remember each day. To our hearts, we say to beat at the right rate and send blood through the arteries for every part of our bodies. Thank you for the filtration system working in proper order as our stomach, kidneys, and intestines speak to one another. All allergies must cease, for you created the earth and everything in it to get along together. Dry up infections in the respiratory system and sinus cavity. We lay hands on the areas of our bodies where we have any pain or infirmity, commanding it to go in the name of Jesus.

Your word rests in our hearts as it says according to 1 Peter 2:21-25: *"For even hereunto were ye called: because Christ also suffered for us, leaving us an example, that ye should follow his steps: who did no sin, neither was guile found in his mouth: who, when he was reviled, reviled not again; when he suffered, he threatened not; but committed himself to him that judgeth righteously: who his own self bare our sins in his own body on the tree, that we, being dead to sins, should live unto righteousness: by whose stripes ye were healed. For ye were as sheep going astray; but are now returned unto the Shepherd and Bishop of your souls."*

We take authority over everything that tries to rise and take control in our lives. It is in the name of Jesus that we pray. Amen.

Stimulating Thought

Are you walking in the victory that God gave you or still giving in to the schemes of Satan? Jesus paid it all when he died, was buried, and rose again. Satan has no more power over our lives than what we give to him. Stand up in the authority that has been given to you and speak to the obstacles that arise. If we believe that we are speaking beings like the God who created us, then what we speak will manifest. Open your mouth and declare what you expect. Look for results because God honors his word.

Reflections

_____

_____

_____

_____

Day 67

Great morning, God. Great morning, Jesus. Great morning, Holy Spirit. Thank you, God, for this day that you have made, and we are glad and rejoicing in it. Forgive us, God, for the things we have said, done, thought, and felt that are not pleasing to you nor lining up with your word.

We give thanks to you, Lord, for you are good and worthy of all our praise. Sharpen our discernment, hearing, and sight. Take us deeper into the oracles and reveal greater revelation to us. Ground and root us so deep in your word that every move we make will release an anointing and leave the residue of your presence.

Build up our faith so that as we minister in the lives of others, your power will work even as we simply pass by them, ushering in miracles, signs, and wonders without even laying hands on anyone. Let healing take place even as we embrace one another so we will feel you through hugs.

Thank you for uncommon favor resting upon us as blessings manifest in our lives. We accept all that your word says concerning our lives, not eliminating or discounting any of it. Philippians 1:14-28 (NIV) tells us: *"And because of my chains, most of the brothers and sisters have become confident in the Lord and dare all the more to proclaim the gospel without fear. It is true that some preach Christ out of envy and rivalry, but others out of goodwill. The latter do so out of love, knowing that I am put here for the defense of the gospel. The former preach Christ out of selfish ambition, not sincerely, supposing that they can stir up trouble for me while I am in chains. But what does it matter? The important thing is that in every way, whether from false motives or true, Christ is preached. And because of this I rejoice. Yes, and I will continue to rejoice, for I know that through your prayers and God's provision of the Spirit of Jesus Christ what has happened to me will turn out for my deliverance. I eagerly expect and hope that I will in no way be ashamed, but will have sufficient courage so that now as always Christ will be exalted in my body, whether by life or by death. For to me, to live is Christ and to die is gain. If I am to go on living in the body, this will mean fruitful labor for me. Yet what shall I choose? I do not know! I am torn between the two: I desire to depart and be with Christ, which is better by far; but it is more necessary for you that I remain in the body. Convinced of this, I know that I will remain, and I will continue with all of you for your progress and joy in the faith, so that through my being with you again your boasting in Christ Jesus will abound on account of me. Whatever happens, conduct yourselves in a manner worthy of the gospel of Christ. Then, whether I come and see you or only hear about you in my absence, I will know that you stand firm in the one Spirit, striving together as one for the faith of the gospel without being frightened in any way by those who oppose you. This is a sign to them that they will be destroyed, but that you will be saved—and that by God."*

The word of truth is welling up inside of us. Prepare our hearts to receive what you are speaking in this hour. Let the word be for us as well as those we will share it with. Thank you for the noticeable change resulting from hearing and responding as you speak the instructions. It is in the name of Jesus we pray. Amen.

Stimulating Thought

Have you ever faced a devastating storm that the meteorologists gave warnings about so that you got all your things prepared and had a supply on hand for a worst-case scenario? Of course, we have all been in that situation in the various regions where we live, for different types of storms have come. What about the storms of life that the chief meteorologists—God, Jesus, and the Holy Spirit—have warned you about? They have even given you the supplies you need to ride out the storm through prayer, praise, worship, and the word. Are you taking and using the supplies or are you trying to do it your own way? Some things in life are bigger than what you can handle in your own strength. Let God do it by leading and guiding you through safely. The aftereffects can be far worse than the storm itself. God already sees down the road what will take place. Follow his lead to end up in the right place after the storm is over.

Reflections

_____

_____

_____

_____

_____

_____

_____

Day 68

Great morning, God. Great morning, Jesus. Great morning, Holy Spirit. Thank you, God, for this day that you have made, and we are glad and rejoicing in it. Forgive us, God, for the things we have said, done, thought, and felt that are not pleasing to you nor lining up with your word.

We say "Yes" today, Lord, to your will for our lives. Thank you for the plan you have set for our lives and for the great things you have in store for us. You have assigned certain people to our lives and certain tasks for our hands to complete. Help us not despise what you have for us to do. Give us wisdom and strategies to get all things done with grace. We stand tall today in the full power and authority that you have given to us. Today we make declarations into the atmosphere and look for those things to manifest.

Keep our minds at peace today and let us be anxious for nothing. No good thing will you withhold from us when we come asking in faith. Thank you for what you have spoken according to your word in Mark 11:22-26: *"And Jesus answering saith unto them, Have faith in God. For verily I say unto you, That whosoever shall say unto this mountain, Be thou removed, and be thou cast into the sea; and shall not doubt in his heart, but shall believe that those things which he saith shall come to pass; he shall have whatsoever he saith. Therefore I say unto you, What things soever ye desire, when ye pray, believe that ye receive them, and ye shall have them. And when ye stand praying, forgive, if ye have ought against any: that your Father also which is in heaven may forgive you your trespasses. But if ye do not forgive, neither will your Father which is in heaven forgive your trespasses."*

Purify our hearts and minds so that your Holy Spirit will have free course in our lives. We need you in every area of our lives, so there is nothing that we try to seal off from you actively being a part of. The possibilities in our lives are limitless when we open up and allow you to do a work in us. We desire to be the best that we can and to be who you said we are, with help from you, heavenly Father. It is in the name of Jesus that we do pray. Amen.

Stimulating Thought

Do you know the power of using words like "I can" and "I will"? If you are not currently saying those phrases, exercise that power by using them—beginning today—and see how different life is for just a day by changing your vocabulary. Remove words from your menu of speech like "I can't," "They won't (or don't)," and "It's not possible to get that done." The word of God tells us that we can do all things through Christ who gives us strength because greater is he who is in us than our enemy. Know the word and live it. There is power in the words that we release—to give life or take it. Choose the words that give life.

Reflections

_____

_____

_____

Day 69

Great morning, God. Great morning, Jesus. Great morning, Holy Spirit. Thank you, God, for this day that you have made, and we are glad and rejoicing in it. Forgive us, God, for the things we have said, done, thought, and felt that are not pleasing to you nor lining up with your word.

We are blessed to still be alive and well. Each day that we spend in your presence is sweeter. God, you are amazing and we are grateful to you for allowing us the many benefits in life. Today is a brand-new day full of great opportunities that you have created for us to use. Holy Spirit, rise in us to speak, to do, and to go where we are needed today to encourage others.

Build up our trust in you as we take our eyes off what man is doing. You have smiled upon us and made us free. Our hearts meditate on your word according to Psalm 18:1-7: *"I will love thee, O Lord, my strength. The Lord is my rock, and my fortress, and my deliverer; my God, my strength, in whom I will trust; my buckler, and the horn of my salvation, and my high tower. I will call upon the Lord, who is worthy to be praised: so shall I be saved from mine enemies. The sorrows of death compassed me, and the floods of ungodly men made me afraid. The sorrows of hell compassed me about: the snares of death prevented me. In my distress I called upon the Lord, and cried unto my God: he heard my voice out of his temple, and my cry came before him, even into his ears. Then the earth shook and trembled; the foundations also of the hills moved and were shaken, because he was wroth."*

Reestablish the things that need to be built back up and effective in our lives. Reconcile and restore relationships that have been altered or distorted by illusions presented by Satan. Give us a greater appreciation for the life you've granted us. You owe us nothing, God, for you have done more than enough for us. We honor you, God. It is in the name of Jesus that we do pray. Amen.

Stimulating Thought

Be determined in all things that you do. God has placed talent in every one of us, but we have to be intentional about completing the tasks. Make up your mind to do what you are passionate about. Continue to speak it until you see it manifest. Position yourself with others who desire to see you succeed and whom you likewise wish to succeed. Separate yourself from negative thinkers because it will take you longer to arrive at your destination when you carry them.

Reflections

_____

_____

_____

_____

_____

_____

_____

Day 70

Great morning, God. Great morning, Jesus. Great morning, Holy Spirit. Thank you, God, for this day that you have made, and we are glad and rejoicing in it. Forgive us, God, for the things we have said, done, thought, and felt that are not pleasing to you nor lining up with your word.

Lord, give us a praying spirit to pray your heart and your will into existence. Decrease our flesh and increase your Spirit within us. Sharpen our discernment and tune our ears to hear your voice clearly.

Eliminate all thoughts that would cause us to doubt or deviate from the truth. We meditate on your word according to Hebrews 3:1-9: *"Wherefore, holy brethren, partakers of the heavenly calling, consider the Apostle and High Priest of our profession, Christ Jesus; who was faithful to him that appointed him, as also Moses was faithful in all his house. For this man was counted worthy of more glory than Moses, inasmuch as he who hath builded the house hath more honour than the house. For every house is builded by some man; but he that built all things is God. And Moses verily was faithful in all his house, as a servant, for a testimony of those things which were to be spoken after; but Christ as a son over his own house; whose house are we, if we hold fast the confidence and the rejoicing of the hope firm unto the end. Wherefore (as the Holy Ghost saith, To day if ye will hear his voice, harden not your hearts, as in the provocation, in the day of temptation in the wilderness: when your fathers tempted me, proved me, and saw my works forty years."*

Direct our steps to keep us on the paths of righteousness and to not deviate from where we should travel. Regulate our minds by casting down every vain imagination that tries to rise. Build up our confidence in the word to daily decree and declare what your word promises for our lives until we see full manifestation. Let confession of the word come forth so that we will live what we speak. Restore the flavor of the salt within us as seasoning for the earth. It is in the name of Jesus that we pray. Amen.

Stimulating Thought

Do you find yourself at a standstill over the opinions that others have of you? We should care what people think of us, but even more we should care how God feels about our lives. When God gives you instructions for life, do it no matter what. He will get a point across through you or someone else. Man does not have a heaven or hell to place us in. God will not have us do anything to appear like a fool.

Reflections

_____

_____

_____

_____

_____

_____

_____

Great morning, God. Great morning, Jesus. Great morning, Holy Spirit. Thank you, God, for this day that you have made, and we are glad and rejoicing in it. Forgive us, God, for the things we have said, done, thought, and felt that are not pleasing to you nor lining up with your word.

We receive your forgiveness today and cast down any vain imagination or foolish thought that leads to sin. Purify our hearts and whatever rests there from thoughts that have lingered. Deliver us from ourselves and the things that sow into our flesh and do not edify growth of our spirit man.

Strengthen us in areas of weakness to pray earnest and fervent prayers from a pure place. Let us not release words in prayer from a selfish posture but from a righteous position as your humble servants. Your word is true and we act accordingly as it says in Psalm 63:1-11: *"O God, thou art my God; early will I seek thee: my soul thirsteth for thee, my flesh longeth for thee in a dry and thirsty land, where no water is; to see thy power and thy glory, so as I have seen thee in the sanctuary. Because thy lovingkindness is better than life, my lips shall praise thee. Thus will I bless thee while I live: I will lift up my hands in thy name. My soul shall be satisfied as with marrow and fatness; and my mouth shall praise thee with joyful lips: when I remember thee upon my bed, and meditate on thee in the night watches. Because thou hast been my help, therefore in the shadow of thy wings will I rejoice. My soul followeth hard after thee: thy right hand upholdeth me. But those that seek my soul, to destroy it, shall go into the lower parts of the earth. They shall fall by the sword: they shall be a portion for foxes. But the king shall rejoice in God; every one that sweareth by him shall glory: but the mouth of them that speak lies shall be stopped."*

Thank you for the things you show us as we simply speak your word over every situation in our lives. We receive correction and deliverance to go forward in the victory that you have already ordained for our lives. There is power in the blood and name of Jesus, neither of which ever weakens or changes. Our trust is built upon the foundation of your word. It is in Jesus's name we do pray. Amen.

Stimulating Thought

God is so amazing and he proves his love for us over and over again. He keeps on blessing us regularly. Are we recognizing and acknowledging the blessings of the Lord? Not the houses and cars but the true day-to-day blessings he sends, such as the people he has placed in our lives. Tell God "Thank you" for all things. Embrace the mind of Christ dwelling within you and the simple things like the air we breathe and having limbs that work and blood flowing in our bodies. Watch your seasons change due to your obedience and gratitude to God for who he is.

Reflections

_____

_____

_____

_____

_____

_____

_____

_____

Day 72

Great morning, God. Great morning, Jesus. Great morning, Holy Spirit. Thank you, God, for this day that you have made, and we are glad and rejoicing in it. Forgive us, God, for the things we have said, done, thought, and felt that are not pleasing to you nor lining up with your word.

Thank you for waking us up with your hand's touch of love to say, "Rise again, my sons and daughters." We are grateful for the sound of the natural orchestra that played as the chime for the internal alarm clock of the earth. Lord, you are the lover of our souls as you keep watch over us day and night. You work miracles every day in our lives and right before our eyes. Set our hearts and minds on things above so that we will not fall to various temptations.

Build up our faith and confidence in your word, God. Strengthen us according to your word in Isaiah 45:18-23: *"For thus saith the Lord that created the heavens; God himself that formed the earth and made it; he hath established it, he created it not in vain, he formed it to be inhabited: I am the Lord; and there is none else. I have not spoken in secret, in a dark place of the earth: I said not unto the seed of Jacob, Seek ye me in vain: I the Lord speak righteousness, I declare things that are right. Assemble yourselves and come; draw near together, ye that are escaped of the nations: they have no knowledge that set up the wood of their graven image, and pray unto a god that cannot save. Tell ye, and bring them near; yea, let them take counsel together: who hath declared this from ancient time? who hath told it from that time? have not I the Lord? and there is no God else beside me; a just God and a Saviour; there is none beside me. Look unto me, and be ye saved, all the ends of the earth: for I am God, and there is none else. I have sworn by myself, the word is gone out of my mouth in righteousness, and shall not return, That unto me every knee shall bow, every tongue shall swear."*

Thank you, Lord, for the oath you took that is higher than any other ever made. We lift your name up before men in all that we do because you are the author and finisher of our faith. There is none like you in all the earth and no one can do the things that you do for us. Thank you for your love, power, and peace that you give to us. It is in the name of Jesus we pray. Amen.

Stimulating Thought

Have you checked your hearing lately? What sounds are you hearing? Is it your voice, the voice of Satan, or the voice of God that you hear most in your life? The results you are consistently seeing in your life can sometimes point to what or whom you are listening to. All the negative thoughts are not coming from God. Satan is not going to tell you anything that will be a permanent blessing in your life. His job is to kill, steal, and destroy, so he has to sow seeds to eventually bring about death in your life. Jesus came that we might have life more abundantly. Accept what God is speaking by yielding to his instructions no matter what.

Reflections

_____

_____

Day 73

Great morning, God. Great morning, Jesus. Great morning, Holy Spirit. Thank you, God, for this day that you have made, and we are glad and rejoicing in it. Forgive us, God, for the things we have said, done, thought, and felt that are not pleasing to you nor lining up with your word.

We thank you today for the blood of Jesus that was shed and is still covering us now. There is power in the blood and the name of Jesus. Open our hearts and minds to receive everything you are sending today. You are not the author of confusion but a God of order, so we bind all confusion now in the name of Jesus.

Let our words be seasoned as salt with grace and not misinterpreted by hearers. Lord, we honor you and your word given to us to live by. We apply the word to our lives according to 2 Corinthians 4:1-9 (NLT): *"Therefore, since God in his mercy has given us this new way, we never give up. We reject all shameful deeds and underhanded methods. We don't try to trick anyone or distort the word of God. We tell the truth before God, and all who are honest know this. If the Good News we preach is hidden behind a veil, it is hidden only from people who are perishing. Satan, who is the god of this world, has blinded the minds of those who don't believe. They are unable to see the glorious light*

of the Good News. They don't understand this message about the glory
of Christ, who is the exact likeness of God. You see, we don't go around
preaching about ourselves. We preach that Jesus Christ is Lord, and we
ourselves are your servants for Jesus' sake. For God, who said, 'Let there
be light in the darkness,' has made this light shine in our hearts so we
could know the glory of God that is seen in the face of Jesus Christ. We
now have this light shining in our hearts, but we ourselves are like frag-
ile clay jars containing this great treasure. This makes it clear that our
great power is from God, not from ourselves. We are pressed on every side
by troubles, but we are not crushed. We are perplexed, but not driven
to despair. We are hunted down, but never abandoned by God. We get
knocked down, but we are not destroyed."

Revive and rejuvenate the areas of our lives that have come to a
standstill. Ignite the fire within us to get up and move in the things
of God. It is not our desire to sleep on you, God, because you are
always there for us. Even when you are silent, you are yet with us.
Help us in the times when we simply need to be quiet and let you
talk to us or on our behalf. Not everything in life warrants a comment from us, and we thank you for having all the answers. It is in
the name of Jesus we pray. Amen.

Stimulating Thought

Are you justified by your faith to feel like you are validated and
qualified for all that God has set for you to do? It does not matter
what people say about or do to you, but rather what matters is where
your faith lies. God has called every person to do something in life,
no matter how big or small the task may seem. Your level of faith to
get it done makes all the difference in the world. You may not have
some official piece of paper that allows you to serve in your current
capacity, but if God has anointed you to do it, that is all that matters.
As with Nehemiah, don't let any Sanballat come to call you down off
the wall for the project God has given you. Identify the people who

are in your corner for you to accomplish your goals in life. Cut off those who constantly bring distractions because they are on assignment from Satan to stop you.

Reflections

_____

_____

_____

_____

_____

_____

_____

Day 74

Great morning, God. Great morning, Jesus. Great morning, Holy Spirit. Thank you, God, for this day that you have made, and we are glad and rejoicing in it. Forgive us, God, for the things we have said, done, thought, and felt that are not pleasing to you nor lining up with your word.

God, you are the joy and strength of our lives every day that we live and breathe. You save, deliver, and heal all things. Father, we come this morning in the name of Jesus on behalf of the many souls around the world today. Touch stony hearts this day to become as flesh.

Open our understanding as you pour out revelation knowledge. Give us the interpretation of the dreams and visions that you send. Discipline us to know when to release what you have revealed and when to keep it quiet. Take away all anxiety and worry today as we give everything to you confidently in prayer. Let the word according to 1 Peter 5:6-11 settle in our spirits: *"Humble yourselves therefore under the mighty hand of God, that he may exalt you in due time: casting all your care upon him; for he careth for you. Be sober, be vigilant; because your adversary the devil, as a roaring lion, walketh about, seeking whom he may devour: whom resist steadfast in the faith, knowing that the same afflictions are accomplished in your brethren that are in the world. But the God of all grace, who hath called us unto his eternal glory by Christ Jesus, after that ye have suffered a while, make you perfect, stablish, strengthen, settle you. To him be glory and dominion for ever and ever. Amen."*

Take away any complacency in us until we come up to the full measure you have given us to use. Stir us up until everything in us becomes alive and active to be used with zeal. Ignite the flames of your Holy Ghost that have died down. We have great expectations this day. It is in the name of Jesus we pray. Amen.

Stimulating Thought

Why do we continue to press through our daily routines when our bodies and spirits crave rest? God has a way to give us the rest we need when we are not wise enough to take it. Our bodies often tell us when they need rest, but we keep going like the Energizer Bunny. Don't wait until God sits you down to rest because you are so exhausted, out of energy, or sick. Take the time to care for yourself. It may be hard at times, and some people don't know how to take care of themselves anymore because of caring for everyone else. There are limitations our bodies can take. Take heed to the signs of danger so that you don't go beyond the point of allowing the body to refresh. God came that we might have life and have it more abundantly. That does include rest.

Reflections

_____

_____

_____

_____

Day 75

Great morning, God. Great morning, Jesus. Great morning, Holy Spirit. Thank you, God, for this day that you have made, and we are glad and rejoicing in it. Forgive us, God, for the things we have said, done, thought, and felt that are not pleasing to you nor lining up with your word.

We love you this morning, Lord. We honor you and give you glory. We exalt you, Father God, for being good and being God all by yourself. God, you are the joy and strength of our lives. You are our peace. Thank you for being our healer and provider.

When all hope seems to be gone and there is no place to turn, you are there fathering us. God, you are so good that we desire to apply Psalm 100:1-5 to our lives: *"Make a joyful noise unto the Lord, all ye lands. Serve the Lord with gladness: come before his presence with singing. Know ye that the Lord he is God: it is he that hath made us, and not we ourselves; we are his people, and the sheep of his pasture. Enter into his gates with thanksgiving, and into his courts with praise: be thankful unto him, and bless his name. For the Lord is good; his mercy is everlasting; and his truth endureth to all generations."*

Reveal some new things to us this day as our eyes are open and our ears are tuned to you. Place a word in our mouth that will set the captives free as we speak life over everyone and every situation today. Let us leave people in better shape when we walk away from them than when we greeted them. As we go through this day, impart to us the things you see our spirits have need of. It is in the name of Jesus that we pray. Amen.

Stimulating Thought

We know that God's grace is sufficient for our lives, but have you ever stopped to think about why God has given us grace? Grace is the love and mercy given to us by God simply because it is his desire that we have it. There is nothing we have done to earn it. It is a spontaneous gift from God to man that no work or effort is put forth to achieve. Often it is undeserved but it is granted to us anyway. Consider the gift of grace before acting or speaking on anything.

Reflections

_____

_____

_____

_____

_____

_____

_____

Day 76

Great morning, God. Great morning, Jesus. Great morning, Holy Spirit. Thank you, God, for this day that you have made, and we are glad and rejoicing in it. Forgive us, God, for the things we have said, done, thought, and felt that are not pleasing to you nor lining up with your word.

It is a brand-new day that we are thankful for, and the old things are passed away. Show us your new mercies this day and cover us with your infinite grace. Lord, refresh us as you send the rains to water the dry places in our lives.

Open our eyes of understanding and sharpen our discernment to recognize the snares and traps the enemy has laid to hold us captive. Give us insight and depth perception to know where to step to avoid danger and what to say to bypass conflict. We receive your word to sink deep into our spirits according to 1 Peter 4:7-19 (NLT): *"The end of the world is coming soon. Therefore, be earnest and disciplined in your prayers. Most important of all, continue to show deep love for each other, for love covers a multitude of sins. Cheerfully share your home with those who need a meal or a place to stay. God has given each of you a gift from his great variety of spiritual gifts. Use them well to serve one another. Do you have the gift of speaking? Then speak as though God himself were speaking through you. Do you have the gift of helping others? Do it with all the strength and energy that God supplies. Then everything you do will bring glory to God through Jesus Christ. All glory and power to him forever and ever! Amen. Dear friends, don't be surprised at the fiery trials you are going through, as if something strange were happening to you. Instead, be very glad—for these trials make you partners with Christ in his suffering, so that you will have the wonderful joy of seeing his glory when it is revealed to all the world. If you are insulted because you bear the name of Christ, you will be blessed, for the glorious Spirit of God rests upon you. If you suffer, however, it must not be for murder, stealing, making trouble, or prying into other people's affairs. But it is no shame to suffer for being a Christian. Praise God for the privilege of being called by his name! For the time has come for judgment, and it must begin with God's household. And if judgment begins with us, what terrible fate awaits those who have never obeyed God's Good News? And also, 'If the righteous are barely saved, what will happen to godless sinners?' So if you are suffering in a manner that pleases God, keep on doing what is right, and trust your lives to the God who created you, for he will never fail you."*

Thank you, Jesus, for being the risen, true, and living Savior that we serve. Let the word sink deep within our spirits until application takes place. Let the world get a glimpse of God when they look at us because of the word filling and flowing from us. It is in the name of Jesus that we pray. Amen.

Stimulating Thought

Have you ever watched little children when they are tired and need a nap? Did you notice their inability to walk and move with coordination—how they wobble and stumble instead? They can't even keep their emotions intact, as they cry and whine while trying to avoid the very thing that the body desperately needs at that moment: rest. We are the same way when our spirits get tired and weary from making wise spiritual decisions. Emotionally we become imbalanced and don't act in the best manner possible. It is so good to know that Jesus extends to us the ability to come to him—all of us who labor and are heavy laden—and he will give us rest. It is awesome to know that he will rescue us in a matter as simple as rest.

Reflections

_____

_____

_____

_____

_____

_____

_____

Day 77

Great morning, God. Great morning, Jesus. Great morning, Holy Spirit. Thank you, God, for this day that you have made, and we are glad and rejoicing in it. Forgive us, God, for the things we have said, done, thought, and felt that are not pleasing to you nor lining up with your word.

Most gracious and almighty God, we come before you this morning with humble hearts and gratitude for allowing us another day to serve you. You are the only living God—the only one to do what you do for us. Thank you for combating sin, sickness, and death on our behalf by sending Jesus to die in our place. Increase our power as we tap into your Holy Spirit for more. We are sensitive to your voice, Father God, and we will not deviate at the voice of Satan. Build us up in our most holy faith today to accomplish everything you have assigned our hands to do. Reveal to us the hidden things and every ambush the enemy has set for us to fall into.

Keep us attentive to the vices of hate and unforgiveness that Satan uses to keep us separate and not as one cohesive body of Christ. Let the word according to Romans 12:9-21 marinate in our spirits: *"Let love be without dissimulation. Abhor that which is evil; cleave to that which is good. Be kindly affectioned one to another with brotherly love; in honor preferring one another; not slothful in business; fervent in spirit; serving the Lord; rejoicing in hope; patient in tribulation; continuing instant in prayer; distributing to the necessity of saints; given to hospitality. Bless them which persecute you: bless, and curse not. Rejoice with them that do rejoice, and weep with them that weep. Be of the same mind one toward another. Mind not high things, but condescend to men of low estate. Be not wise in your own conceits. Recompense to no man evil for evil. Provide things honest in the sight of all men. If it be possible, as much as lieth in you, live peaceably with all men. Dearly beloved, avenge not yourselves, but rather give place unto wrath: for it is written, Vengeance is mine; I will repay, saith the Lord. Therefore if thine enemy hunger, feed him; if he thirst, give him drink: for in so doing thou shalt heap coals of fire on his head. Be not overcome of evil, but overcome evil with good."*

Work on our temperament for good fruit to be produced to draw others to you, God, based on our actions and speech. God, we love you, and we love everyone and everything you created in the earth. May the love we have win the souls that are held captive. It is in the name of Jesus that we pray. Amen.

Stimulating Thought

Are you taking time each day to make sure you are well kept? We know that God keeps us, but are you keeping yourself well balanced in every area as you should? Do you get the proper rest that your body requires daily? Are you eating a balanced diet for your body to gain the nutrients it needs and what is helpful for total body functionality? Are you exercising to keep everything in good running condition as it should be? Consider doing all these things to take the best care of your body, as well as taking mental breaks to have a clear mind. Read the word to feed your spirit what it needs to grow. In all of this, make sure to love yourself because God made you the way you are. So be sure to also love others in the state they are in right now. It may be your love that pulls someone out of the bad place they are in right now in life.

Reflections

_____

_____

_____

_____

_____

_____

_____

Day 78

Great morning, God. Great morning, Jesus. Great morning, Holy Spirit. Thank you, God, for this day that you have made, and we are glad and rejoicing in it. Forgive us, God, for the things we have said, done, thought, and felt that are not pleasing to you nor lining up with your word.

We come with great expectation and anticipation this brand-new day that you have presented to us. Open our thinking to receive the revelation you are giving. Our hearts yearn for an encounter with you like never before as we come seeking your face and embracing the move of your Holy Spirit. Take us to that secret place to have uninterrupted worship with you, Father God.

Give us the strategies and steps to move through the traps and devices set for us by the enemy. Raise our spiritual antennas to tap into what your Spirit is speaking in response to conditions in the earth. Renew our strength and restore our joy to complete every task placed before us this day. The word according to Proverbs 3:19-33 brings comfort to our soul: *"The Lord by wisdom hath founded the earth; by understanding hath he established the heavens. By his knowledge the depths are broken up, and the clouds drop down the dew. My son, let not them depart from thine eyes: keep sound wisdom and discretion:*

so shall they be life unto thy soul, and grace to thy neck. Then shalt thou walk in thy way safely, and thy foot shall not stumble. When thou liest down, thou shalt not be afraid: yea, thou shalt lie down, and thy sleep shall be sweet. Be not afraid of sudden fear, neither of the desolation of the wicked, when it cometh. For the Lord shall be thy confidence, and shall keep thy foot from being taken. Withhold not good from them to whom it is due, when it is in the power of thine hand to do it. Say not unto thy neighbor, Go, and come again, and to morrow I will give; when thou hast it by thee. Devise not evil against thy neighbor, seeing he dwelleth securely by thee. Strive not with a man without cause, if he have done thee no harm. Envy thou not the oppressor, and choose none of his ways. For the froward is abomination to the Lord: but his secret is with the righteous. The curse of the Lord is in the house of the wicked: but he blesseth the habitation of the just."

Quicken our spirits to agree and comply with your word. Let us not justify or participate in anything that might seem right but does not line up with your standard of holiness. Give us boldness in all that we do for there to be a Holy Ghost takeover in every setting we find ourselves today. Step in, God, for there to be balance where it is needed in our lives. Humble us before you so that all the glory is given to you. There is nothing we can do in our own strength unless you place it in us to do everything we need to get done. It is in the name of Jesus we pray. Amen.

Stimulating Thought

Have you ever lost your composure over something and you recognized after the fact that the enemy tried to get your day off track? His job is to steal, kill, and destroy at any cost. Prepare yourself to beat the enemy at his own game. Pray often and repent for both the things you know that you did wrong and anything else you may not be aware of. Ask God to seal off every crack that the enemy may attempt to enter through to have a stronghold in your life. Be open to what God is doing in you and remain humble. That may sometimes mean saying "I'm sorry" when you didn't do anything wrong but you simply need be the bigger person in the situation for the God in you to rise up and for enemies to scatter. Even when God is sharpening our discernment by showing us things in one another that are not lining up, we cannot get frazzled and twisted by what we see. Stay calm and simply pray for God to work it out and for deliverance to come. God is always teaching us lessons, but are we being attentive students to learn the material, retain the knowledge, and pass the test?

Reflections

Day 79

Great morning, God. Great morning, Jesus. Great morning, Holy Spirit. Thank you, God, for this day that you have made, and we are glad and rejoicing in it. Forgive us, God, for the things we have said, done, thought, and felt that are not pleasing to you nor lining up with your word.

Give us clean hearts and minds. Purify the thoughts we entertain. Refresh us in the areas of our lives where we have become complacent and stagnant. Spirit of the living God, fall fresh upon us. Shape and mold us in the areas that need to be enhanced in our lives. Open us up to hear and see things from a different perspective and receive what you intend for us.

Refocus us as we meditate on and fulfill your word according to Colossians 1:9-17: *"For this cause we also, since the day we heard it, do not cease to pray for you, and to desire that ye might be filled with the knowledge of his will in all wisdom and spiritual understanding; that ye might walk worthy of the Lord unto all pleasing, being fruitful in every good work, and increasing in the knowledge of God; strengthened with all might, according to his glorious power, unto all patience and longsuffering with joyfulness; giving thanks unto the Father, which hath made us meet to be partakers of the inheritance of the saints in light: who hath delivered us from the power of darkness, and hath translated us into the kingdom of his dear Son: in whom we have redemption through his blood, even the forgiveness of sins: who is the image of the invisible God, the firstborn of every creature: for by him were all things created, that are in heaven, and that are in earth, visible and invisible, whether they be thrones, or dominions, or principalities, or powers: all things were created by him, and for him: and he is before all things, and by him all things consist.*"

Remove every obstacle and every stumbling block that keeps our spirits from growing. Take away the aspects of our opinion that block us from being obedient to what you instruct, God. Our desire is to worship you in spirit and in truth. It is in the name of Jesus that we do pray. Amen.

Stimulating Thought

Have you ever heard people say that a cluttered desk belongs to a person with a cluttered mind? There can often be some truth in that statement. Sometimes when people have a hard time putting external things in their proper places, it correlates to things being out of place in their inner lives as well. For some people, it may be a matter of simply adhering to structure and order in their lives. With others, it may be learning to let go of old things for new material to come into their lives. Whatever the case, face reality when your life gets crowded. When we see clutter in our natural lives, there is clutter in our spirits. We are holding on to false burdens and carrying things God did not intend for us to carry. He said for us to cast our cares upon him. Just let go, starting today. Empty those meaningless and unnecessary things into both the natural and spiritual garbage cans so that they will no longer clutter up and be hazardous to your life because of what might be attracted to hide within the clutter.

Reflections

_____

_____

_____

_____

_____

_____

_____

Day 80

Great morning, God. Great morning, Jesus. Great morning, Holy Spirit. Thank you, God, for this day that you have made, and we are glad and rejoicing in it. Forgive us, God, for the things we have said, done, thought, and felt that are not pleasing to you nor lining up with your word.

We offer a sacrifice of praise to you, Lord, for your goodness and mercy. Strengthen us in areas of our lives where we are weak today. In a posture of humility, we revere you, almighty God. You are awesome, God, and we are grateful for every miracle you perform in our lives each day. Thank you for the simple things in life like oxygen and the flow of blood in our bodies necessary for us to live.

Excitement, joy, and expectation fill the air today as we think about the goodness of Jesus and what he has in store for our lives. Thank you for a time of reflection as we seek your face. Speak to our spirits, for we are open to receive what you desire to release. Manifest results as we stand on your word for change in us according to Ezekiel 36:23-30 (NKJV): *"And I will sanctify My great name, which has been profaned among the nations, which you have profaned in their midst; and the nations shall know that I am the Lord,' says the Lord God, 'when I am hallowed in you before their eyes. For I will take you from among the nations, gather you out of all countries, and bring you into your own land. Then I will sprinkle clean water on you, and you shall be clean; I will cleanse you from all your filthiness and from all your idols. I will give you a new heart and put a new spirit within you; I will take the heart of stone out of your flesh and give you a heart of flesh. I will put My Spirit within you and cause you to walk in My statutes, and you will keep My judgments and do them. Then you shall dwell in the land that I gave to your fathers; you shall be My people, and I will be your God. I will deliver you from all your uncleannesses. I will call for the grain and multiply it, and bring no famine upon you. And I will multiply the fruit of your trees and the increase of your fields, so that you need never again bear the reproach of famine among the nations.'"*

Take away all guilt and shame of our past actions as we stand up in newness to be who you have made us today. Shine your light on every area of our lives to expose any darkness illegally attached so we can break free. It is in the name of Jesus we pray. Amen.

Stimulating Thought

Tune your ears and focus your thoughts today as God gives you details for his strategic plans to improve your life. Opportunities are opening and increase is coming. Prepare yourself for their arrival. Do not be afraid when something good happens because it seems unreal. God always wants to give the best to his children. Recondition your thoughts to receive what God allows you to have. Sometimes we are our own worst critics in life because we don't feel that we deserve to have the blessings. Everything in this earth belongs to God and he decides how to disperse what he has made. His blessings make us rich and he adds no sorrow to them. So what if you made a mistake or bad choice in the past! Repent, accept God's forgiveness, and move on. God loves us so much that he is always waiting to bless us.

Reflections

_____

_____

_____

_____

_____

_____

_____

Day 81

Great morning, God. Great morning, Jesus. Great morning, Holy Spirit. Thank you, God, for this day that you have made, and we are glad and rejoicing in it. Forgive us, God, for the things we have said, done, thought, and felt that are not pleasing to you nor lining up with your word.

We have a feeling of breaking forth in our spirits today, for we know that greater things are coming our way. Pour out your Spirit, Lord, and send the anointing that will destroy yokes. Penetrate our hearts today with your word. Let it cut deep to deliver us from any blockages or clots in our spiritual bloodstream that might hinder the church from functioning as it should.

Demonstrate your power as we worship you in spirit and truth for miracles, signs, and wonders to follow. We thank you for the results that manifest in our lives as we soak in the word according to 1 Kings 8:54-61: *"And it was so, that when Solomon had made an end of praying all this prayer and supplication unto the Lord, he arose from before the altar of the Lord, from kneeling on his knees with his hands spread up to heaven. And he stood, and blessed all the congregation of Israel with a loud voice, saying, Blessed be the Lord, that hath given rest unto his people Israel, according to all that he promised: there hath not failed one word of all his good promise, which he promised by the hand of Moses his servant. The Lord our God be with us, as he was with our fathers: let him not leave us, nor forsake us: that he may incline our hearts unto him, to walk in all his ways, and to keep his commandments, and his statutes, and his judgments, which he commanded our fathers. And let these my words, wherewith I have made supplication before the Lord, be nigh unto the Lord our God day and night, that he maintain the cause of his servant, and the cause of his people Israel at all times, as the matter shall require: that all the people of the earth may know that the Lord is God, and that there is none else. Let your heart therefore be perfect with the Lord our God, to walk in his statutes, and to keep his commandments, as at this day."*

Thank you for protecting our hearts by writing your word upon the tablets of our hearts as we read and chew on the word to digest into our spirits. Take away any malice, strife, envy, jealousy, or offense we have held on to in regard to past things so that it will not eat away at our consciences. Restore the happiness and joy that have disappeared from many of us, and refresh those who are stagnant. It is in the name of Jesus we pray. Amen.

Stimulating Thought

When was the last time you had a spiritual reboot? So many of our electrical devices have computer processors within—like cell phones, tablets, desktops, laptops, etc.—and it is necessary to power them off occasionally for the systems to reset and run smoothly again. When these systems shut down temporarily, it allows updates to take effect upon restart, as well as to clear errors or interruptions in the system. For the most effective functioning of your own systems, it is recommended to reboot at least once a day. As you look over your day-to-day life, do you take the necessary time to reboot daily for God to send the updates you need? Be refreshed with a restart each day as you go before the Lord and allow him to download into your spirit.

Reflections

_____

_____

_____

_____

_____

_____

_____

Day 82

Great morning, God. Great morning, Jesus. Great morning, Holy Spirit. Thank you, God, for this day that you have made, and we are glad and rejoicing in it. Forgive us, God, for the things we have said, done, thought, and felt that are not pleasing to you nor lining up with your word.

Most gracious Father in heaven, we come before you humbled and in a posture of submission. Thank you for being the great I Am in our lives. Thank you for being Jehovah Jireh to provide all our needs, no matter when or where we need them. You are Jehovah Rapha, healer of every infirmity in our lives, and for that we are eternally grateful.

Let the word sink deep within us as Psalm 34:1-19 expresses: *"I will bless the Lord at all times: his praise shall continually be in my mouth. My soul shall make her boast in the Lord: the humble shall hear thereof, and be glad. O magnify the Lord with me, and let us exalt his name together. I sought the Lord, and he heard me, and delivered me from all my fears. They looked unto him, and were lightened: and their faces were not ashamed. This poor man cried, and the Lord heard him, and saved him out of all his troubles. The angel of the Lord encampeth round about them that fear him, and delivereth them. O taste and see that the Lord is good: blessed is the man that trusteth in him. O fear the Lord, ye his saints: for there is no want to them that fear him. The young lions do lack, and suffer hunger: but they that seek the Lord shall not want any good thing. Come, ye children, hearken unto me: I will teach you the fear of the Lord. What man is he that desireth life, and loveth many days, that he may see good? Keep thy tongue from evil, and thy lips from speaking guile. Depart from evil, and do good; seek peace, and pursue it. The eyes of the Lord are upon the righteous, and his ears are open unto their cry. The face of the Lord is against them that do evil, to cut off the remembrance of them from the earth. The righteous cry, and the Lord heareth, and delivereth them out of all their troubles. The Lord is nigh unto them that are of a broken heart; and saveth such as be of a contrite spirit. Many are the afflictions of the righteous: but the Lord delivereth him out of them all."*

Your word is your bond and we can depend on what you have spoken, God. You faithfully reign on the throne over all the earth, God. Great things are coming today and we are excited about the move you are making in the earth. It is in the name of Jesus we pray. Amen.

Stimulating Thought

Are you being the best you possibly can be? There is so much potential inside of every single person God created. Do something with what God gave you instead of allowing your gifts and talents to go stale and dry up. Ask God how to use what you possess, then use it for his glory. Make new discoveries about yourself each day as God reveals more of himself to you. Don't wait for permission from others to be who God called you to be. Don't even look to be validated by others when God has given you a vision and instructions to carry out. Be the best *you* every day of your life so that when you leave this earth, you will go out empty.

Reflections

_____

_____

_____

_____

_____

_____

_____

Day 83

Great morning, God. Great morning, Jesus. Great morning, Holy Spirit. Thank you, God, for this day that you have made, and we are glad and rejoicing in it. Forgive us, God, for the things we have said, done, thought, and felt that are not pleasing to you nor lining up with your word.

Lord, we love you because you first loved us. You are worthy of all glory, honor, and praise. Thank you for the promises that you have made and thank you for keeping them. You are able to do everything you said you would do. Your love and patience do not give up on us.

We stand firm on every word you have spoken, because your word is true and makes us free. Our prayer for all of mankind is according to Romans 10:1-13: *"Brethren, my heart's desire and prayer to God for Israel is, that they might be saved. For I bear them record that they have a zeal of God, but not according to knowledge. For they being ignorant of God's righteousness, and going about to establish their own righteousness, have not submitted themselves unto the righteousness of God. For Christ is the end of the law for righteousness to every one that believeth. For Moses describeth the righteousness which is of the law, That the man which doeth those things shall live by them. But the righteousness which is of faith speaketh on this wise, say not in thine heart, Who shall ascend into heaven? (that is, to bring Christ down from above:) or, Who shall descend into the deep? (that is, to bring up Christ again from the dead.) But what saith it? The word is nigh thee, even in thy mouth, and in thy heart: that is, the word of faith, which we preach; that if thou shalt confess with thy mouth the Lord Jesus, and shalt believe in thine heart that God hath raised him from the dead, thou shalt be saved. For with the heart man believeth unto righteousness; and with the mouth confession is made unto salvation. For the scripture saith, Whosoever believeth on him shall not be ashamed. For there is no difference between the Jew and the Greek: for the same Lord over all is rich unto all that call upon him. For whosoever shall call upon the name of the Lord shall be saved."*

Thank you for placing a heart in us to believe and receive your plan to redeem us. Our cry today is for lost souls to be free from torment and anguish. When you made us, we were created for your glory and to be with you eternally. Hell is not our home or final destination, because you created it for the devil and his angels. So touch hearts all over the world to line up with your will for our lives so that we all arrive at the place you prepared for us and intended for us to spend eternity. It is in the name of Jesus we pray. Amen.

Stimulating Thought

As mentioned in a previous devotional, we often hear the cliché, "The mind is a terrible thing to waste." That is true but let's go a step further with that thought: our lives are a terrible thing to waste. God created everyone with a plan in mind for their lives. He gives us choices and does not force us to do anything. Greatness is in all of us because we've been made fearfully and wonderfully by God and he said we are good. When we entertain all kinds of thoughts and are open to anything, it sinks down into our spirits. Our spirits lead our flesh, but sometimes we are exposed to things that contaminate our spirits and then the flesh takes over. Be careful with what you take in from day to day to feed your body, mind, and spirit. If all you eat is junk, you can get sick, become malnourished, and possibly not grow and mature. Feed your mind and spirit a proper diet of the word, prayer, and worship to have a thriving and healthy life. Get God—it does a life good.

Reflections

Day 84

Great morning, God. Great morning, Jesus. Great morning, Holy Spirit. Thank you, God, for this day that you have made, and we are glad and rejoicing in it. Forgive us, God, for the things we have said, done, thought, and felt that are not pleasing to you nor lining up with your word.

We bless you, Lord, with all our soul, and all that is within us blesses you. Your grace and mercy are unmatched by anything or anyone in the earth. Lord, we come humbled before you as we make supplication on behalf of man today. Touch hearts and minds today for change to come. Purify our hearts and intentions as we come before you so that we will see a manifestation of results after we have prayed.

Let there be increase in our spirits as you pour out upon us today. Rise in us, Holy Spirit, to do great exploits in the earth that will leave the world astonished at the move of God. Shake the foundations and loose the chains of tradition that many people are bound by. Destroy the walls of fear that confine us to certain activities. Let the word according to 1 Peter 4:1-14 (NLT) sink deep into our spirits: *"So then, since Christ suffered physical pain, you must arm yourselves with the same attitude he had, and be ready to suffer, too. For if you have suffered physically for Christ, you have finished with sin. You won't spend the rest of your lives chasing your own desires, but you will be anxious to do the will of God. You have had enough in the past of the evil things that godless people enjoy—their immorality and lust, their feasting and drunkenness and wild parties, and their terrible worship of idols. Of course, your former friends are surprised when you no longer plunge into the flood of wild and destructive things they do. So they slander you. But remember that they will have to face God, who stands ready to judge everyone, both the living and the dead. That is why the Good News was preached to those who are now dead—so although they were destined to die like all people, they now live forever with God in the Spirit. The end of the world is coming soon. Therefore, be earnest and disciplined in your prayers. Most important of all, continue to show deep love for each other, for love covers a multitude of sins. Cheerfully share your home with those who need a meal or a place to stay. God has given each of you a gift from his great variety of spiritual gifts. Use them well to serve one another. Do you have the gift of speaking? Then speak as though God himself were speaking through you. Do you have the gift of helping others? Do it with all the strength and energy that God supplies. Then everything you do will bring glory to God through Jesus Christ. All glory and power to him forever and ever! Amen. Dear friends, don't be surprised at the fiery trials you are going through, as if something strange were happening to you. Instead, be very glad—for these trials make you partners with Christ in his suffering, so that you will have the wonderful joy of seeing his glory when it is revealed to all the world. If you are insulted because you bear the name of Christ, you will be blessed, for the glorious Spirit of God rests upon you."*

The cost you paid for our debt, Jesus, will forever remain unreimbursed because we cannot repay the fee, nor have you required settlement. Thank you for being an awesome God investing at such a high risk, already knowing the odds of any return. We are reminded every day that there is nothing impossible for you to do in each of our lives. Use us for your glory in all that we do, and set a watch upon our lips so that nothing unclean will proceed from our mouths. It is in the name of Jesus we pray. Amen.

Stimulating Thought

Are you effectively speaking words that give life in every situation you are presented with, or are you killing with your choice of words? To receive the response you are looking for, ask God to give you the words to say before you release them into the atmosphere. The more of his word you digest, the more your vocabulary will reflect the image of God in your life. Don't cut off your ability to digest the word by spitting it out. Swallow it and accept the nutrients it gives.

Reflections

Day 85

Great morning, God. Great morning, Jesus. Great morning, Holy Spirit. Thank you, God, for this day that you have made, and we are glad and rejoicing in it. Forgive us, God, for the things we have said, done, thought, and felt that are not pleasing to you nor lining up with your word.

Strengthen us today in our minds to retain the word of the Lord, for you remind us, Holy Spirit, of every word that God has spoken. Keep us in all our ways as we fervently stay before you in prayer. Set the agenda for our day for your perfect will to be done in our lives today and every day.

Grant us the peace we need to endure opposition and obstacles that rise in our lives. We are blessed to know that before a thing even begins, we have victory when we ask, because you said in your word according to 1 John 5:1-15: *"Whosoever believeth that Jesus is the Christ is born of God: and every one that loveth him that begat loveth him also that is begotten of him. By this we know that we love the children of God, when we love God, and keep his commandments. For this is the love of God, that we keep his commandments: and his commandments are not grievous. For whatsoever is born of God overcometh the world: and this is the victory that overcometh the world, even our faith. Who is he that overcometh the world, but he that believeth that Jesus is the Son of God? This is he that came by water and blood, even Jesus Christ; not by water only, but by water and blood. And it is the Spirit that beareth witness, because the Spirit is truth. For there are three that bear record in heaven, the Father, the Word, and the Holy Ghost: and these three are one. And there are three that bear witness in earth, the Spirit, and the water, and the blood: and these three agree in one. If we receive the witness of men, the witness of God is greater: for this is the witness of God which he hath testified of his Son. He that believeth on the Son of God hath the witness in himself: he that believeth not God hath made him a liar; because he believeth not the record that God gave of his Son. And this is the record, that God hath given to us eternal life, and this life is in his Son. He that hath the Son hath life; and he that hath not the Son of God hath not life. These things have I written unto you that believe on the name of the Son of God; that ye may know that ye have eternal life, and that ye may believe on the name of the Son of God. And this is the confidence that we have in him, that, if we ask any thing according to his will, he heareth us: and if we know that he hear us, whatsoever we ask, we know that we have the petitions that we desired of him."*

Kindle the fire in us to pray without ceasing, and open our spirits to worship you freely without limits or boundaries. Unlock the destiny within us, stir us up, and reveal gifts we have not yet discovered to be used for your glory. Shake up the thirst, hunger, and desire within us for more of your word and Spirit. Pour it out, God, in the increments that we are capable of receiving to satisfy our taste. Let our prayers be as walls formed around cities to fortify against the blows of the enemy. Calm our minds and give us indescribable peace so that nothing will shake our faith. It is well with our souls today, for we are in agreement with you and your word, God. In the name of Jesus we do pray. Amen.

Stimulating Thought

As we continually say we want more from the Lord, what are we doing to actively gain it? Growth is a natural process in life, but it requires eating, resting, and some movement. Daily we must eat of the word of God for our spirits and minds to grow beyond the stage of infancy. Even after growing, some development has to take place. Flex your spiritual muscles of faith to see the strength of the word at work as you apply it to your life each day. Be still from time to time as you hear what the Lord is speaking for your life at the "rest areas" where he allows you to regroup. Hit the ground running when he instructs you to go. As you run the race, you get faster, stronger, wiser, and more powerful. Embrace all that the Lord has for your life.

Reflections

_____

_____

_____

_____

_____

_____

_____

Day 86

Great morning, God. Great morning, Jesus. Great morning, Holy Spirit. Thank you, God, for this day that you have made, and we are glad and rejoicing in it. Forgive us, God, for the things we have said, done, thought, and felt that are not pleasing to you nor lining up with your word.

Father, we come this morning with praise upon our lips and a heart of worship for you. Anoint us afresh until we are dripping with favor to flow over into the lives of others. We seek you early this morning while you may be found, so speak the instructions, Lord, and set our agenda for today. We believe you, God, and trust you with all our hearts. In all our ways we acknowledge you. You said you would never leave or forsake us, for you are with us always.

Stir up the creative abilities within us to think on new ideas and witty inventions. Wake up and resurrect what you have placed inside of us that we have suppressed and not used. Fear and intimidation have no rule over us from this day forward because we have an appointment with destiny that they are not invited to. Thank you for manifestation of your word in our lives according to Ephesians 1:4-18 (NLT): *"Even before he made the world, God loved us and chose us in Christ to be holy and without fault in his eyes. God decided in advance to adopt us into his own family by bringing us to himself through Jesus Christ. This is what he wanted to do, and it gave him great pleasure. So we praise God for the glorious grace he has poured out on us who belong to his dear Son. He is so rich in kindness and grace that he purchased our freedom with the blood of his Son and forgave our sins. He has showered his kindness on us, along with all wisdom and understanding. God has now revealed to us his mysterious will regarding Christ—which is to fulfill his own good plan. And this is the plan: At the right time he will bring everything together under the authority of Christ—everything in heaven and on earth. Furthermore, because we are united with Christ, we have received an inheritance from God, for he chose us in advance, and he makes everything work out according to his plan. God's purpose was that we Jews who were the first to trust in Christ would bring praise and glory to God. And now you Gentiles have also heard the truth, the Good News that God saves you. And when you believed in Christ, he identified you as his own by giving you the Holy Spirit, whom he promised long ago. The Spirit is God's guarantee that he will give us the inheritance he promised and that he has purchased us to be his own people. He did this so we would praise and glorify him. Ever since I first heard of your strong faith in the Lord Jesus and your love for God's people everywhere, I have not stopped thanking God for you. I pray for you constantly, asking God, the glorious Father of our Lord Jesus Christ, to give you spiritual wisdom and insight so that you might grow in your knowledge of God. I pray that your hearts will be flooded with light so that you can understand the confident hope he has given to those he called—his holy people who are his rich and glorious inheritance."*

Keep us focused as we walk on the straight and narrow paths to arrive on time at our destined place. Revive the zeal within us as we press toward the mark for prize of the high calling in Jesus. Thank you in advance for results today. Our faith is such that everything we speak into the atmosphere will happen today. Salvation is coming in the lives of people around the world in places that have rejected you, God. There shall be deliverance for the captives bound in their minds and spirits. Healing is manifesting in our physical bodies, amazing even medical professionals. We yield and are sensitive to you, Holy Spirit. It is in the name of Jesus we pray. Amen.

Stimulating Thought

Have you ever looked back over your life and thought about the places and things that God has brought you out of? When we stop to think it over, we have all had some close calls in our lives and some tough places we have been in. But the Lord is faithful. God is always watching over us no matter where we are and what we are doing. It does not even matter who we are with; he still watches over us. Just evaluate for a minute how you felt some of those times when you were in a tough spot. There were probably even times you thought you wouldn't make it. But the Lord is faithful. I sometimes remind myself of how many times my life could have gone another way and I could even be dead because of the things I have faced in my life. But the Lord is faithful. Think on that every time you want to complain about how hot it is outside. Think on that every time you want to complain about the rain. Think on that every time you murmur about what is not right in your life instead of what is right. You are still here. Would you have the alternative *right now* of death and not deal with what takes place in the earth? Enjoy what God sends every day and ask him what you should learn from this.

Reflections

_____

_____

_____

_____

_____

Day 87

Great morning, God. Great morning, Jesus. Great morning, Holy Spirit. Thank you, God, for this day that you have made, and we are glad and rejoicing in it. Forgive us, God, for the things we have said, done, thought, and felt that are not pleasing to you nor lining up with your word.

Humble our hearts this morning and let your will be done in us. Break up the fallow ground for seeds to be planted and penetrate. Thank you for a harvest coming forth after you have cultivated our hearts to produce good.

We embrace your word today according to 2 Chronicles 15:1-13: *"And the Spirit of God came upon Azariah the son of Oded: and he went out to meet Asa, and said unto him, Hear ye me, Asa, and all Judah and Benjamin; The Lord is with you, while ye be with him; and if ye seek him, he will be found of you; but if ye forsake him, he will forsake you. Now for a long season Israel hath been without the true God, and without a teaching priest, and without law. But when they in their trouble did turn unto the Lord God of Israel, and sought him, he was found of them. And in those times there was no peace to him that went out, nor to him that came in, but great vexations were upon all the inhabitants of the countries. And nation was destroyed of nation, and city of city: for God did vex them with all adversity. Be ye strong therefore, and let not your hands be weak: for your work shall be rewarded. And when Asa heard these words, and the prophecy of Oded the prophet, he took courage, and put away the abominable idols out of all the land of Judah and Benjamin, and out of the cities which he had taken from mount Ephraim, and renewed the altar of the Lord, that was before the porch of the Lord. And he gathered all Judah and Benjamin, and the strangers with them out of Ephraim and Manasseh, and out of Simeon: for they fell to him out of Israel in abundance, when they saw that the Lord his God was with him. So they gathered themselves together at Jerusalem in the third month, in the fifteenth year of the reign of Asa. And they offered unto the Lord the same time, of the spoil which they had brought, seven hundred oxen and seven thousand sheep. And they entered into a covenant to seek the Lord God of their fathers with all their heart and with all their soul; that whosoever would not seek the Lord God of Israel should be put to death, whether small or great, whether man or woman."*

Our alliance is with you, God, concerning all things in our lives. Shield us from every plot and device Satan has set against us. Cancel the thoughts that are fostered by Satan and then rise in our minds against you, God. Keep us engaged in and focused on your word. Develop us to remain in agreement with you, God, and to stay on task to arrive at the appointed place we need to reach in life. Work out every detail for our good, even if we are uncomfortable as you do it. We know you have our best interest at heart. It is in the name of Jesus that we pray. Amen.

Stimulating Thought

Who are you in agreement with, or who have you formed an alliance with in your life? Throughout history we see relationships of allies formed between families, tribes, nations, and even man and God. The strongest ally anyone can have is God, because he watches over all the earth and has power over everything to move on our behalf.

As long as you are in agreement with God, no harm can come to you because no weapon formed against you shall prosper. Our covenant with God is sealed by the blood of Jesus, and we can always depend on him. We can form agreements with people from all walks of life and in many high positions, but none will protect us like God does. Think about the possible repercussions of making allegiances with people you don't know, especially when you don't know what they stand for.

Reflections

_____

_____

_____

_____

_____

_____

Day 88

Great morning, God. Great morning, Jesus. Great morning, Holy Spirit. Thank you, God, for this day that you have made, and we are glad and rejoicing in it. Forgive us, God, for the things we have said, done, thought, and felt that are not pleasing to you nor lining up with your word.

Prepare our hearts and minds for all that we shall face today. Set the agenda for our day to go according to your plan for us rather than the path our flesh wants to take. Calm our spirits of all fear and chaos as we strategically conquer every adversity that arises. Hide us so deep in your word that we must seek you to find ourselves.

Give us revelation like never before as you unlock treasures hidden in the oracles of your word. Your word boldly establishes your position in our lives according to Isaiah 43:15-19: *"I am the Lord, your Holy One, the creator of Israel, your King. Thus saith the Lord, which maketh a way in the sea, and a path in the mighty waters; which bringeth forth the chariot and horse, the army and the power; they shall lie down together, they shall not rise: they are extinct, they are quenched as tow. Remember ye not the former things, neither consider the things of old. Behold, I will do a new thing; now it shall spring forth; shall ye not know it? I will even make a way in the wilderness, and rivers in the desert."*

Stretch us in prayer as your Holy Spirit prays through us. Thank you for what you have in store for us, for you have already predestined our lives. Nothing can stop what you have already assigned to bless our lives. We praise you in advance simply because we are grateful for life and for you being our Lord. It is in the name of Jesus that we pray. Amen.

Stimulating Thought

As you are transitioning from one phase to another in your life, do you sometimes find yourself in a foreign place unfamiliar to you? As we grow and mature, we stretch out into uncharted territory to make new discoveries in life that cannot be found in the places we left behind. While there, we are reminded that Jesus is our rock in a weary land. He is the only stable thing no matter where we land in life. So always remember: Jesus does not change; it is we who change our posture.

Reflections

_____

_____

_____

_____

_____

_____

_____

Day 89

Great morning, God. Great morning, Jesus. Great morning, Holy Spirit. Thank you, God, for this day that you have made, and we are glad and rejoicing in it. Forgive us, God, for the things we have said, done, thought, and felt that are not pleasing to you nor lining up with your word.

Humble our hearts and bring peace to our spirits. Calm us down where needed. Rise in us, Holy Spirit, for God to get glory out of our lives. Heal every hurt and mend all that is broken.

Set a watch upon our lips for edifying and encouraging words to come from us. Let the word according to Proverbs 18:1-15 (GNT) settle in our spirits for change to manifest: *"People who do not get along with others are interested only in themselves; they will disagree with what everyone else knows is right. A fool does not care whether he understands a thing or not; all he wants to do is show how smart he is. Sin and shame go together. Lose your honor, and you will get scorn in its place. A person's words can be a source of wisdom, deep as the ocean, fresh as a flowing stream. It is not right to favor the guilty and keep the innocent from receiving justice. When some fool starts an argument, he is asking for a beating. When a fool speaks, he is ruining himself; he gets caught in the trap of his own words. Gossip is so tasty—how we love to swallow it! A lazy person is as bad as someone who is destructive. The Lord is like a strong tower, where the righteous can go and be safe. Rich people, however, imagine that their wealth protects them like high, strong walls around a city. No one is respected unless he is humble; arrogant people are on the way to ruin. Listen before you answer. If you don't, you are being stupid and insulting. Your will to live can sustain you when you are sick, but if you lose it, your last hope is gone. Intelligent people are always eager and ready to learn."*

Help our ears to hear things in the entire context before we offer a response in situations not requiring an answer or our opinion. Resolve offenses that arise so that peace will be the result. Thank you, God, for causing us to face those personal giants that we have overlooked or avoided in our lives rather than allow you to deliver us from them. This day we stand before you transparent because change is desired for our lives. We want to be whole in our bodies, minds, and spirits. It is in the name of Jesus we pray. Amen.

Stimulating Thought

We like to think that as we get older, we grow wiser. That is not always the case. Wisdom comes from God. He said if anyone lacks wisdom to ask of him. Fear of the Lord is the beginning of wisdom. We have to dig deeper in the word to even know what to ask God. Have you tried digging deeper into the things of God but then felt like you hit rock or hard clay that stopped you from digging further? God never told us it would be easy, but it is worth it in the end. Continue to dig and to seek him. Reward does come.

Reflections

_____

_____

_____

_____

_____

_____

_____

Day 90

Great morning, God. Great morning, Jesus. Great morning, Holy Spirit. Thank you, God, for this day that you have made, and we are glad and rejoicing in it. Forgive us, God, for the things we have said, done, thought, and felt that are not pleasing to you nor lining up with your word.

You bless us every day over and over again without hesitation. Your grace and mercy surround each of us daily, allowing us to obtain everything we need to sustain our lives. Open our eyes to see your truth at all times and to not follow after things that are false. Guard and guide our tongues so that wrong words will not proceed from our mouths. Place words in us that will build up and edify everyone we encounter.

Sharpen our eyes of discernment to recognize what you are showing us, and give us wisdom to know what to do with what we are shown. We chew on the word according to 1 Corinthians 2:4-14: *"And my speech and my preaching was not with enticing words of man's wisdom, but in demonstration of the Spirit and of power: that your faith should not stand in the wisdom of men, but in the power of God. Howbeit we speak wisdom among them that are perfect: yet not the wisdom of this world, nor of the princes of this world, that come to nought: but we speak the wisdom of God in a mystery, even the hidden wisdom, which God ordained before the world unto our glory: which none of the princes of this world knew: for had they known it, they would not have crucified the Lord of glory. But as it is written, Eye hath not seen, nor ear heard, neither have entered into the heart of man, the things which God hath prepared for them that love him. But God hath revealed them unto us by his Spirit: for the Spirit searcheth all things, yea, the deep things of God. For what man knoweth the things of a man, save the spirit of man which is in him? even so the things of God knoweth no man, but the Spirit of God. Now we have received, not the spirit of the world, but the spirit which is of God; that we might know the things that are freely given to us of God. Which things also we speak, not in the words which man's wisdom teacheth, but which the Holy Ghost teacheth; comparing spiritual things with spiritual. But the natural man receiveth not the things of the Spirit of God: for they are foolishness unto him: neither can he know them, because they are spiritually discerned."*

Cleanse us to the point that your Spirit will find nothing but what pleases you deep in us. We yield to the move of your Holy Spirit in our lives. Purge our hearts of anything illegally resting there that might negatively influence our thoughts. Open our minds to receive what you have for us. It is in the name of Jesus we pray. Amen.

Stimulating Thought

God is well able to do everything in our lives if we let him. Why then do we continue with the struggles we face from day to day in our lives if God is willing and able to do what we need? God desires for us to be free of the things that hinder us from moving forward with a prosperous life. It begins with us being confident in our relationship with him to know who we are in God. Never settle for anything less than giving your very best for God to work with.

Reflections

_____

_____

_____

_____

_____

_____

_____

About the Author

Tiwana L. Adams has served in many capacities in the local church. Her primary ministry gifts lie in intercessory prayer and teaching the word of God. God has endowed her with a prayer mantle that requires not only prayer for the local body of Christ, but he has called her to the forefront to intercede on behalf of nations.

Wearing many hats as wife, mother, friend, minister, author and founder of a non-profit, her most cherished role is child of the God. As a woman of faith, she is committed to fulfilling her assignment for life. She feels that there is good in everyone and they just need an opportunity for it to come out. She works diligently to impact the kingdom by teaching, unlocking, stirring up the gifts and sharpening others so that they can confidently operate in the grace upon their lives.

Tiwana has a great passion for the word of God and desires to be an encourager to all that she meets daily. Her personal desire is to share a life changing word that will compel the sinner to receive salvation and to shed light in the lives of God's people to change their course forever more for the Glory of our Lord and Savior Jesus Christ! Resting on Psalm 119:130, "The entrance of thy words giveth light; it giveth understanding unto the simple," as her motto for life . . . for men to be drawn to Christ.

Connect

If you enjoyed this book, please purchase copies for your loved ones and leave a review on Amazon.com.

Connect with the author on social media:
Instagram - @tadams0629
Facebook - https://www.facebook.com/tiwana.adams/

Made in the USA
Columbia, SC
14 May 2021